Levinas and the Philosophy of Education

Delving into Levinas's ideas in nuanced and sophisticated ways, this book innovatively blends and juxtaposes Levinas with other thinkers, perspectives, and fields of thinking. Some contributions are traditional, but superbly analyzed and argued renderings of his thought, and they contrast with more creative readings of Levinas through lenses such as Durkheim, Habermas, feminism, indigenous studies, and new materialism.

This collection will serve to reinvigorate Levinas and the importance of the many facets of his thinking that link to the ethical and lived dimensions of our educational worlds. Readers will find this to be a very interesting, engrossing, and well-thought-out book that forms a vibrant and exciting intervention into the philosophy of education and Levinas studies in general.

This book was originally published as a special issue of *Educational Philosophy and Theory*.

Guoping Zhao is a Professor at Oklahoma State University, USA. She works in the fields of philosophy of education, comparative philosophy, and Chinese education. Her work has focused on theories of the subject, ethics, spirituality, and democracy. She is the co-editor of *Re-Envisioning Chinese Education: The Meaning of Person-Making in a New Age* (with Zongyi Deng, 2015).

Educational Philosophy and Theory

Series Editor: Peter Roberts, University of Canterbury, New Zealand

This series is devoted to cutting-edge scholarship in educational philosophy and theory. Each book in the series focuses on a key theme or thinker and includes essays from a range of contributors. To be published in the series, a book will normally have first appeared as a special issue of *Educational Philosophy and Theory*, one of the premier philosophy of education journals in the world. This provides an assurance for readers of the quality of the work and enhances the visibility of the book in the international philosophy of education community. Books in this series combine creativity with rigour and insight. The series is intended to demonstrate the value of diverse theoretical perspectives in educational discourse, and contributors are invited to draw on literature, art and film as well as traditional philosophical sources in their work. Questions of educational policy and practice will also be addressed. The books published in this series will provide key reference points for subsequent theoretical work by other scholars, and will play a significant role in advancing philosophy of education as a field of study.

Titles in the series include:

New Directions in Educational Leadership Theory
Edited by Scott Eacott and Colin W. Evers

Expertise, Pedagogy and Practice
Edited by David Simpson and David Beckett

Philosophy and Pedagogy of Early Childhood
Edited by Sandy Farquhar and E. Jayne White

The Dilemma of Western Philosophy
Edited by Michael A. Peters and Carl Mika

Educational Philosophy and New French Thought
Edited by David R. Cole and Joff P.N. Bradley

Activating Aesthetics
Edited by Elizabeth M. Grierson

Levinas and the Philosophy of Education
Edited by Guoping Zhao

The Confucian Concept of Learning
Revisited for East Asian Humanistic Pedagogies
Edited by Duck-Joo Kwak, Morimichi Kato and Ruyu Hung

A Kaleidoscopic View of Chinese Philosophy of Education
Edited by Ruyu Hung

John Dewey's Democracy and Education in an Era of Globalization
Edited by Mordechai Gordon and Andrea R. English

Levinas and the Philosophy of Education

Edited by
Guoping Zhao

LONDON AND NEW YORK

First published 2018
by Routledge
2 Park Square, Milton Park, Abingdon, Oxon, OX14 4RN, UK

and by Routledge
711 Third Avenue, New York, NY 10017, USA

Routledge is an imprint of the Taylor & Francis Group, an informa business

Introduction, Chapters 1–3, 5–7 © 2018 Philosophy of Education Society of Australasia
Chapter 4 © 2015 Gert Biesta

With the exception of Chapter 4, no part of this book may be reprinted
or reproduced or utilised in any form or by any electronic, mechanical,
or other means, now known or hereafter invented, including photocopying
and recording, or in any information storage or retrieval system, without
permission in writing from the publishers. For details on the rights for
Chapter 4, please see the chapter's Open Access footnote.

Trademark notice: Product or corporate names may be trademarks or
registered trademarks, and are used only for identification and
explanation without intent to infringe.

British Library Cataloguing in Publication Data
A catalogue record for this book is available from the British Library

ISBN 13: 978-0-8153-5959-3

Typeset in Plantin
by RefineCatch Limited, Bungay, Suffolk

Publisher's Note
The publisher accepts responsibility for any inconsistencies that may have
arisen during the conversion of this book from journal articles to book chapters,
namely the possible inclusion of journal terminology.

Disclaimer
Every effort has been made to contact copyright holders for their permission to
reprint material in this book. The publishers would be grateful to hear from any
copyright holder who is not here acknowledged and will undertake to rectify
any errors or omissions in future editions of this book.

Contents

Citation Information	vii
Notes on Contributors	ix
Introduction: Levinas and the Philosophy of Education *Guoping Zhao*	1
1. Levinas, Durkheim, and the Everyday Ethics of Education *Anna Strhan*	9
2. Singularity and Community: Levinas and democracy *Guoping Zhao*	24
3. Sound not Light: Levinas and the Elements of Thought *Emma Williams and Paul Standish*	38
4. The Rediscovery of Teaching: On robot vacuum cleaners, non-egological education and the limits of the hermeneutical world view *Gert Biesta*	52
5. The Temporal Transcendence of the Teacher as Other *Clarence W. Joldersma*	71
6. Education Incarnate *Sharon Todd*	83
7. Taking Responsibility into all Matter: Engaging Levinas for the climate of the 21ˢᵗ Century *Betsan Martin*	96
Index	115

Citation Information

The chapters in this book were originally published in *Educational Philosophy and Theory*, volume 48, issue 4 (April 2016). When citing this material, please use the original page numbering for each article, as follows:

Introduction
Levinas and the Philosophy of Education
Guoping Zhao
Educational Philosophy and Theory, volume 48, issue 4 (April 2016) pp. 323–330

Chapter 1
Levinas, Durkheim, and the Everyday Ethics of Education
Anna Strhan
Educational Philosophy and Theory, volume 48, issue 4 (April 2016) pp. 331–345

Chapter 2
Singularity and Community: Levinas and democracy
Guoping Zhao
Educational Philosophy and Theory, volume 48, issue 4 (April 2016) pp. 346–359

Chapter 3
Sound not Light: Levinas and the Elements of Thought
Emma Williams and Paul Standish
Educational Philosophy and Theory, volume 48, issue 4 (April 2016) pp. 360–373

Chapter 4
The Rediscovery of Teaching: On robot vacuum cleaners, non-egological education and the limits of the hermeneutical world view
Gert Biesta
Educational Philosophy and Theory, volume 48, issue 4 (April 2016) pp. 374–392

Chapter 5
The Temporal Transcendence of the Teacher as Other
Clarence W. Joldersma
Educational Philosophy and Theory, volume 48, issue 4 (April 2016) pp. 393–404

CITATION INFORMATION

Chapter 6
Education Incarnate
Sharon Todd
Educational Philosophy and Theory, volume 48, issue 4 (April 2016) pp. 405–417

Chapter 7
Taking Responsibility into all Matter: Engaging Levinas for the climate of the 21ˢᵗ Century
Betsan Martin
Educational Philosophy and Theory, volume 48, issue 4 (April 2016) pp. 418–436

For any permission-related enquiries please visit:
http://www.tandfonline.com/page/help/permissions

Notes on Contributors

Gert Biesta is Professor of Education at Brunel University, London, UK. His work focuses on the theory of education and the theory and philosophy of educational and social research, with a particular interest in relationships between education and democracy. His latest book is *The Beautiful Risk of Education* (2014).

Clarence W. Joldersma is Professor of Education at Calvin College, USA, where he teaches philosophy of education. His recent books include *A Levinasian Ethics for Education's Commonplaces* (2014) and the edited volume *Neuroscience and Education: A Philosophical Appraisal* (2016).

Betsan Martin led the establishment of United Nations University Waikato Center of Expertise in Education for Sustainable Development at the University of Waikato, New Zealand. The Centre is co-governed with Māori. Betsan is involved with programmes in the Pacific region, and is Chair of the International Alliance for Responsible and Sustainable Societies.

Paul Standish is Professor and Head of the Centre for Philosophy of Education at University College London, UK. He is interested particularly in tensions between analytical and continental philosophical traditions and the creative possibilities that arise from them. He is the co-editor of *Education and the Kyoto School of Philosophy* (with Naoko Saito, 2012).

Anna Strhan is a Fellow in the Department of Religious Studies at the University of Kent, UK. Her research interests lie in the interrelations between religion, ethics, meaning, and modernity. She is the author of *Levinas, Subjectivity, Education: Towards an Ethics of Radical Responsibility* (2012) and *Aliens and Strangers?: The Struggle for Coherence in the Everyday Lives of Evangelicals* (2015).

Sharon Todd is Professor of Education at Maynooth University, Ireland. She is author of *Learning from the Other: Levinas, Psychoanalysis, and Ethical Possibilities in Education* (2003) and *Toward an Imperfect Education: Facing Humanity, Rethinking Cosmopolitanism* (2009). She is the co-editor of *Re-imagining Relationships in Education: Ethics, Politics and Practices* (with Morwenna Griffiths, Marit Honerød Holveid, and Christine Winter, 2015).

Emma Williams is an Assistant Professor in the Centre for Education Studies, University of Warwick, UK. Her work explores the themes of language, rationality, and subjectivity within the context of education. She is the author of *The Ways We Think* (2016).

NOTES ON CONTRIBUTORS

Guoping Zhao is a Professor at Oklahoma State University, USA. She works in the fields of philosophy of education, comparative philosophy, and Chinese education. Her work has focused on theories of the subject, ethics, spirituality, and democracy. She is the co-editor of *Re-Envisioning Chinese Education: The Meaning of Person-Making in a New Age* (with Zongyi Deng, 2015).

INTRODUCTION

Levinas and the Philosophy of Education

GUOPING ZHAO

Emmanuel Levinas, one of the most profoundly original Western philosophers in the twentieth century, has recently received considerable attention from educators and educational theorists. Against the Western convention that centers human subjectivity on the all-encompassing power of ego and consciousness, Levinas locates the origin of the subject in the pre-ego, pre-conscious connection with the Other and the world. The imprint of, and the self's responsibility to, the Other break open the enclosed identity and entail a formation of the subject that is open, transcendental, and ethical. Levinas's account of human subjectivity has addressed many of the problems of modern Western philosophy. Not only has he escaped the metaphysical tradition of Being as fixed presence, but he has also provided a completely new understanding of the Other that is not divided from, and cannot be objectified by, the subject, but is an irreplaceable part of the constitution of the subject. He has truly deconstructed the modern subject, which has been under attack for so long but had yet to be dismantled.

Levinas's philosophy is deeply rooted in the post-WWII anti-totalitarian thought of continental philosophy. After the devastation and upon the wreckage of the last century, continental philosophy mounted a formidable challenge to totalitarianism, essentialism, and fundamentalism, which have dominated modern philosophy since the Enlightenment. German critical thinkers and French post-modern and post-structural philosophers have all traced the root of totalitarianism to false identity thinking (Adorno, 1990), or in Levinas's words, the logic of the same, that presents a picture of exhaustive identity and presence at the cost of difference and absence. In France, this challenge has evolved into the so-called philosophy of difference that concerns itself centrally with difference and its valorization (May, 1997). While totalitarianism is the movement of reducing the other to the same either by eliminating or by absorbing the other, the philosophy of difference attempts to show the very irreducibility of otherness and the very impossibility of total sameness and presence. As a key figure in this movement, Levinas spotlights the irreducibility of the otherness of the Other both within and outside of the subject and the Other's ability to break out of the grip of knowledge and concepts, and its constitutive power that leaves an indelible mark on the very 'presence' and 'identity' that is to be forged by our consciousness. In many ways, the anti-totalitarianism movement has irreversibly shattered much of the foundation upon which modern Western philosophy is built. It is no longer possible, for example, to use identity thinking to overcome or compromise human diversity and still be philosophically justified when we approach people of difference.

LEVINAS AND THE PHILOSOPHY OF EDUCATION

However, this anti-totalitarian movement, particularly in the form of postmodern and post-structural thought, has also been frequently criticized as inviting nihilism and relativism and thus as having little application to our social and political lives, including education. In Rikowski's words, 'The insertion of postmodernism within educational discourse lets in some of the most unwelcome guests—nihilism, relativism, educational marketisation, to name but a few—which makes thinking about human emancipation futile' (1996, p. 442). Without getting into the debate on whether postmodernism necessarily leads to nihilism and relativism, it is sufficient for the purpose of this special issue to say that such a critique cannot be launched against Levinas. As May (1997) notes, while it may be true that Foucault and Deleuze 'often resist discussions of ethics altogether—or at least the kind of ethics that has any resonance with the concern for others that has been the hallmark of traditional ethical positions—one's relationship with and responsibility to the other have been the centerpiece of Levinas's thought' (p. 131). Characteristically, Levinas's philosophy can be read as an ontology as well as ethics, and his theory of the subject has been worked out as an ethics (Critchley, 2008). Levinas's work has been the driving force leading to the ethical turn in postmodern and post-structural philosophy. An increasing, deep confluence has been noted in recent years among thinkers such as Jacques Derrida, Jean-Luc Nancy, Jean-François Lyotard, and Levinas (May, 1997). Levinas's influence is enabling continental philosophy to participate more forcefully in our social and political lives and in education. Not only his acute concern with ethics but also his novel idea of human subjectivity make his work essentially relevant to education—a field that is ultimately concerned with the transformation and alteration of human beings.

Other than his essays to the male teachers in a Jewish school where he was the director, published in *Difficult Freedom* (1990), Levinas has not written extensively on education. However, these essays, as well as his occasional mention of teaching and learning in other writings, indicate that his educational ideas were intimately incorporated into his ethical philosophy. He sees teaching as the Other's confrontation with the self, guiding the self in breaking its interiority and going beyond the confines of its nature. In *Totality and Infinity*, Levinas states, '[Teaching] designates an interior being that is capable of a relation with the exterior, and does not take its own interiority for the totality of being' (1969, p. 180). Teaching and learning are about encountering the new and strange, about being interrupted and called into responsibility to the Other.

Educational theorists have been quick to recognize the significance of Levinas's philosophy for education. In fact, Birgit Nordtug (2013) observed a 'turn towards Levinas's ethical perspective' (p. 250) in educational philosophy in recent years. In 2003, the first special issue devoted to Levinas was published by *Studies in Philosophy and Education* based on a 2000 AERA panel presentation. In 2009, the first edited collection specifically to address Levinas and education, *Levinas and Education: At the Intersection of Faith and Reason*, was published by Routledge. Numerous articles on Levinas have been published in almost all major philosophy of education journals, and presentations on Levinas are frequently featured at PES annual meetings. Several books centered on Levinas and education have also appeared in recent years (e.g. Strhan, 2012; Todd, 2003a).

LEVINAS AND THE PHILOSOPHY OF EDUCATION

The welcoming of Levinas to the field of the philosophy of education is situated in the historical context of neoliberalism and the quest for certainty, uniformity, and accountability. Levinas's philosophy gives educational theorists the conceptual tools to resist dominance and to rethink educational theory and practice in ways radically different from modern Western conventions. The areas of education scholars have explored with a Levinasian lens are varied, covering a wide range of educational concerns, from the purpose of education (Biesta, 2009; Zhao, 2012), curriculum issues and pedagogy (Biesta, 2010; Standish, 2008; Winter, 2014), teacher-student relations (Joldersma, 2002; Säfström, 2003), and the educational aim of autonomy as contrary to heteronomy (Kodelja, 2008; Strhan, 2009; Zhao, 2014a), to art education (Zhao, 2014b). Not surprisingly, particular attention has been paid to the ethical implications of Levinas's philosophy for education in areas related to moral education, diversity issues, multiculturalism, and the politics of recognition. His idea that the knowing subject is interrupted and disarmed by the face of the unknowable Other has been taken up quite frequently by educational theorists to envision the school as a site of ethics (e.g. Chinnery, 2003; Todd, 2004).

Throughout the years, there has also been an identifiable trend in the Levinas scholarship in education, developing from an earlier cautious exposition and concern for faithful interpretation to the later more full-blown, critical analysis and creative extension of his ideas. The early concern for faithful exposition comes from the fact that while Levinas's philosophy is incredibly rich and extremely refreshing for educational scholars, it ultimately hinges on a disruption of Being and Presence and on the claim of the impossibility of thematization, and his writing is enigmatic and at times elusive. Unlike some other continental philosophers, Levinas does not shy away from the daunting and dangerous task of articulating something irreducible to concepts and knowledge; thus, his text is often understandably obscure. And since he locates the origin of human subjectivity in the pre-ego, pre-conscious, connection with the Other and the world (Zhao, 2012), applying his work to educational theories and practices is inherently difficult. Therefore, the first questions educational scholars often have to grapple with are 'the question of how to approach the writings of Emmanuel Levinas' (Biesta, 2003, p. 61) and how to 'think alongside Levinas, to think with his inversion of being as an ethical question' (Todd, 2003b, p. 3).

Hence the earlier scholarship on Levinas and education is marked by the struggle to interpret some of Levinas's evasive ideas in a way that is authentic to his intentions, and multiple interpretations of the same idea frequently emerge. Distortions or facile readings of Levinas have been claimed (Standish, 2008), and debates on particular Levinasian themes are part of the scholarship. For example, Levinas's notion of subjectivity is one of his central themes, and scholars such as Biesta and I have been debating different ways to interpret his approach and its implications for education (Zhao, 2012, 2014a).

After more than a decade, the scholarship has become more confident and mature, not in the sense that scholars are able to reach consensus, but in the sense that they no longer tiptoe around Levinas's writings but are more active and comfortable in drawing out Levinas's insights through sympathetic critique and extension to address some of the most pressing socio-political and educational issues of our time. Sharon

Todd in this issue suggests that in order for the hidden significance of some of Levinas's ideas to shine forth, we must take a more active role in engaging from the outside in a conversation with Levinas instead of only explicating from within his 'tightly constrained systems of meaning'. When we engage with Levinas from outside perspectives, wedding his ideas with other schools of thought or placing social and educational demands on his work, clear meanings and logical implications can be elicited from Levinas's system of thought. Through this process of 'dis-placing and re-positioning', we are not creating new ideas 'entirely out of joint with the very trajectory of his thought', but rather we are allowing new nuances and novel relations of ideas to emerge so 'new life is breathed into it' (Todd, this issue).

The present issue is precisely the outcome of such development and maturity in Levinas scholarship in education.[1] Most of the authors were part of the early 'Levinas turn' and have been at the forefront of the Levinas's scholarship in education along the way. Thus it can be expected that this is not a collection of congruent interpretations of Levinas but of disparate and diverse readings and renderings of Levinas's thought to current contexts in education. What distinguishes this issue is the contributors' innovative extensions of his ideas and the productive blending of Levinas with other thinkers, perspectives, and fields of thinking. Readers will see traditional, yet sophisticated and nuanced, renderings of Levinas's thought, but also more creative readings of Levinas through such lens as feminism and the new materialism. This collection will take readers to many exciting new places and serve to reinvigorate Levinas and the importance of the many facets of his thinking for the ethical and lived dimensions of our educational worlds.

The author of the first article, Anna Strhan, has been known as a Levinas scholar for years. She has written extensively on Levinas's ideas of radical responsibility, subjectivity, and heteronomy, exploring the political significance of Levinas's work for contemporary debates on education. In 'Levinas, Durkheim and the Everyday Ethics of Education', Strhan explores the influence of Émile Durkheim on the philosophy of Levinas in order both to open up the political significance of Levinas's thought and to develop more expansive meanings of moral and political community within education. She argues that most scholarship on Levinas has located his work too exclusively within the phenomenological tradition and the result has been a loss of the political significance of his work. Bringing together Durkheim and Levinas, she offers theoretical resources to deepen the understanding of education as the site of an everyday ethics and a prophetic politics opening onto more compelling ideals for education than those dominant within standard educational discourses.

Having attempted to extend several of Levinas's ideas to the context of art education (Zhao, 2014b), discussion on the 'gift of teaching' (Zhao, 2014a), and having worked on a post-humanist notion of subjectivity drawing on Levinas and the philosophy of difference (Zhao, in press), here I bring up the issue of community and democracy in conversation with Levinas's ideas of singularity and multiplicity (see 'Singularity and Community: Levinas and Democracy' in this issue). I argue that Levinas's ideas of singularity and multiplicity and his identification of language and discourse as the ultimate means to create an ethical community provide tangible possibilities for rebuilding genuine democracy in a human world, democracy that does not reduce and compromise our subjectivity. The expressive use of language prioritized by Levinas over its rational use in the forms of speaking and listening enables a humane, ethical relation among singularities. By cultivating and reorienting the way we approach, speak, and listen to others, we can signify and receive each other as unique subjects with whom we engage in communication and rational debate. This view gives us a new way to work with Habermas's communicative democracy with more attention to human differences and uniqueness.

The third article, Paul Standish and Emma Williams's 'Sound not Light: Levinas and the Elements of Thought', extends Levinas's concept of the Other beyond the relation to the other human being to the understanding of human thinking. In this extension of Levinas's philosophy, his account of the face and his claim that the relation to the face is 'heard in language' are taken up and closely examined. Standish is a prominent figure who has already attempted to extend Levinas's idea of the relation to the Other beyond the human face, particularly to the subjects of study, in a book chapter, 'Levinas and the Language of the Curriculum' (Standish, 2008). While addressing the distortions or facile readings of Levinas in the social sciences and education, Standish has advocated 'applying' Levinas to educational practices as opposed to 'undue piety towards [Levinas's] ideas' (Standish, 2008, p. 57). Emma Williams has also been putting Levinas into conversation with other philosophers, drawing on Derrida and Austin in pondering the relationship between language and thought (Williams, 2007, 2014). In this article, Williams and Standish join to explicate what is at stake in Levinas's claim that the relation to the face is 'heard in language'. They show how Levinas's philosophy leads us away from what might be called a tradition of understanding human thought through the medium of light (and hence intellection, theoria, contemplation) and takes us towards a conception of thinking that is conditioned by sound (and hence speech, language, and the sign). The authors argue that such a shift changes the way we understand thinking and the *teaching* of thinking and enables us to do justice to the otherness that conditions thought.

The author of the fourth article, Gert Biesta, is well known for his writings on Levinas's philosophy and its implications for education. He has been instrumental in the turn to Levinas in education, and his influence on Levinas scholarship cannot be underestimated. Biesta's work most centrally focuses on how Levinas's approach to subjectivity has challenged the modern concept of the subject, which according to Biesta underpins modern education. Biesta phrases Levinas's approach in different terms, from 'uniqueness', 'irreplaceability', to the current 'subjectness', to underscore the responsive nature of Levinas's subjectivity. While I have argued against his interpretation of Levinas (Zhao, 2012, 2014a), I appreciate his many initiatives in using Levinas's thought to challenge current educational theory and practices. His propositions of education as 'subjectification' (2009), the 'pedagogy of interruption' (2010), and his recent call to bring teaching back to education (2013) have been highly influential beyond the field of the philosophy of education. In 'The Rediscovery of Teaching: On Robot Vacuum Cleaners, Non-Egological Education, and the Limits of the Hermeneutical Worldview', Biesta uses the striking metaphor of 'robot vacuum cleaners' to provide a fascinating analysis of current education in an attempt to reclaim the place of teaching in education. Biesta argues that the contemporary critique of so-called traditional teaching is rightly leveled at an authoritarian conception of teaching as control, a conception in which the student can only exist as an object of the intervention of the teacher and never as a subject in its own right. However, he argues that the popular alternative to traditional teaching, which is to make the teacher a facilitator of learning, is still insufficient. Biesta suggests that Levinas puts forward the case that our subjectness is not generated through our own acts of signification, but is rather constituted from the outside, that is, through the address of the other. Thus, placing an educational demand on Levinas's system of thought, Biesta proposes a different conception of teaching, one that is aimed at making the subjectness of the student possible.

Clarence Joldersma, author of the fifth article, is also a well-known Levinas scholar and has been part of the Levinas scholarship from the beginning. His recent work systematically applies Levinas's ethics to the commonplaces of education—teaching, learning, curriculum, and instruction—through an interesting analysis of the experiences of calling and inspiration (2014). His article in this issue, 'The Temporal Transcendence of the Teacher as Other', responds to Biesta's call for the return of teaching in education and argues that over the last decades, education has shifted more clearly to a learner-centered understanding, including constructivism in particular, leaving little room conceptually for a substantive role for the teacher. Through a very interesting exploration of Levinas's idea of time as instants (durations) that come to the ego as a gift from the future, he reframes the role of the teacher as the Other and as the transcendent, who makes possible the learning of something new and something not yet contained.

The last two authors make intriguing extensions of Levinas's thought beyond the conventional, humanistic limits. Sharon Todd, who is known for her beautiful writing and sophisticated and rigorous 'thinking along' with Levinas (2003b), creatively blends Levinas's thought with materialism and feminism. In 'Education Incarnate: Assessing What's New with Levinas', she explores Levinas's ideas of sensibility, materiality, and embodiment and argues that they are at the core of Levinas's ethics. Following a feminist and Deleuzian orientation to education, Todd suggests that the human body is not merely the physical counterpart to a self, but part of the very materiality that comprises spaces for subject transformation. Embodiment and sensibility are ethical features of educational life, insofar as educational settings are concerned with the pedagogical transformation of the self. Todd proposes that Levinas's views of sensibility and embodiment are quintessentially pedagogical aspects of his thought—that is, they are always already rooted in a relational context of change and alteration of the subject, a process through which one becomes someone 'beyond' the limits of one's previous incarnation. Todd's writings have been widely cited and some of her phrases, such as 'learning from the other', 'imperfect education', and 'teaching with ignorance' have become catch phrases for educators in understanding current educational conditions. It is expected that this new article will provide additional insights and perhaps a new way of thinking about education.

The author of the last article, Betsan Martin, has been at the forefront of global and institutional efforts for natural conservation and sustainable development. She led the establishment of a United Nation's Center of Expertise in Education for

Sustainable Development and is Chair of the International Alliance for Responsible and Sustainable Societies. Working at the interface of indigenous worldviews and post-anthropocentric ethics, she finds Levinas's idea of responsibility ultimately relevant and attempts to extend Levinas' ethics of responsibility from a human-centered view to include humans as interdependent with nature. Her article, 'Taking Responsibility Into All Matter: Engaging Levinas in Indigenous and Quantum Thought for Matters of the 21th Century', is an exciting blend of Levinas with indigenous worldviews and quantum theory. She argues that, rather than focusing on the idea of 'face' and limiting our responsibility to the human Other, the essence of Levinas's ethics is to break with the totality of being, which enables us to broaden the horizon of the infinite Other to guard against the enclosure in being. She further suggests that Levinasian ethics questions the stronghold of liberal humanistic goals in education and opens up a horizon for the shared destiny of humans and nature—an 'eco-pedagogy'.

All in all, this issue contains an exciting set of diverse, yet complementary papers. With its interesting, engrossing, and well analyzed and argued renderings of Levinas's system of thought, this special issue is expected to make a distinctive and important contribution to the philosophy of education. A very effective and affecting collection, this special issue will, it is hoped, form a vibrant and exciting intervention into not only the philosophy of education but Levinas studies in general, and beyond.[2]

Disclosure statement

No potential conflict of interest was reported by the author.

Notes

1. One side note: The geographic origins of the contributors (Europe, North America, and New Zealand) signal the global presence of the educational interest in Levinas.
2. I would like to express my gratitude to the blind reviewers for their generous comments on this special issue.

References

Adorno, T. W. (1990). *Negative Dialectics*. (E. B. Ashton, Trans.). London: Routledge.
Biesta, G. (2003). Learning from Levinas: A response. *Studies in Philosophy and Education, 22*, 61–68.
Biesta, G. (2009). Good education in an age of measurement: On the need to reconnect with the question of purpose in education. *Educational Assessment, Evaluation and Accountability, 21*, 33–46.
Biesta, G. (2010). Education after the death of the subject: Levinas and the pedagogy of interruption. In Z. Leonardo (Ed.), *The handbook of cultural politics and education* (pp. 289–302). Rotterdam: Sense.

LEVINAS AND THE PHILOSOPHY OF EDUCATION

Biesta, G. (2013). Receiving the gift of teaching: From 'learning from' to 'being taught by'. *Studies in Philosophy and Education, 32,* 449–461.

Chinnery, A. (2003). Aesthetics of surrender: Levinas and the disruption of agency in moral education. *Studies in Philosophy and Education, 22,* 5–17.

Critchley, S. (2008). The split subject. *Journal of Chinese Philosophy, 35,* 79–87.

Joldersma, C. W. (2002). Pedagogy of the other: A Levinasian approach to the teacher-student relationship. In S. Rice (Ed.), *Philosophy of education society yearbook 2001* (pp. 181–188). Urbana: Philosophy of Education Society-University of Illinois.

Joldersma, C. W. (2014). *A Levinasian ethics for education's commonplaces.* New York, NY: Palgrave Pivot.

Kodelja, Z. (2008). Autonomy and heteronomy. In D. Egéa-Kuehne (Ed.), *Levinas and education* (pp. 186–197). London: Routledge.

Levinas, E. (1969). *Totality and infinity.* (A. Lingis, Trans.). Pittsburgh, PA: Duquesne University Press.

Levinas, E. (1990). *Difficult freedom.* (S. Hand, Trans.). Baltimore, MD: John Hopkins University Press.

May, T. (1997). *Reconsidering difference: Nancy, Derrida, Levinas, and Deleuze.* University Park: The Pennsylvania State University Press.

Nordtug, B. (2013). The welcoming of Levinas in the philosophy of education – at the cost of the Other? *Theory and Research in Education, 11,* 250–268.

Rikowski, G. (1996). Left alone: End time for Marxist educational theory? *British Journal of Sociology of Education, 17,* 415–451.

Säfström, C. A. (2003). Teaching otherwise. *Studies in Philosophy and Education, 22,* 19–29.

Standish, P. (2008). Levinas and the language of the curriculum. In D. Egéa-Kuehne (Ed.), *Levinas and education* (pp. 56–66). London: Routledge.

Strhan, A. (2009). *The very subjection of the subject: Levinas, heteronomy and the philosophy of education.* Paper presented at the annual meeting of the Philosophy of Education Society Great Britain. Oxford University, Oxford.

Strhan, A. (2012). *Levinas, subjectivity, education.* Oxford: Wiley-Blackwell.

Todd, S. (2003a). *Learning from the other: Levinas, psychoanalysis and ethical possibilities in education.* Albany: SUNY Press.

Todd, S. (2003b). Introduction: Levinas and education: The question of implication. *Studies in Philosophy and Education, 22*(1), 1–4.

Todd, S. (2004). Teaching with ignorance: Questions of social justice, empathy, and responsible community. *Interchange, 35,* 337–352.

Williams, E. (2007). *Ontological tragedy: An examination of Levinas' early confrontation with Heideggerian ontology.* Coventry: University of Warwick.

Williams, E. (2014). Out of the ordinary: Incorporating limits with Austin and Derrida. *Educational Philosophy and Theory, 46,* 1337–1352.

Winter, C. (2014). Curriculum knowledge, justice, relations: The schools white paper (2010) in England. *Journal of Philosophy of Education, 48,* 276–292.

Zhao, G. (2012). Levinas and the mission of education. *Educational Theory, 62,* 659–675.

Zhao, G. (2014a). Freedom reconsidered: Heteronomy, open subjectivity, and the 'gift of teaching'. *Studies in Philosophy and Education, 33,* 513–525.

Zhao, G. (2014b). Art as alterity in education. *Educational Theory, 64,* 245–259.

Zhao, G. (in press). From the philosophy of consciousness to the philosophy of difference: The subject for education after humanism. *Educational Philosophy and Theory.* doi:10.1080/00131857.2015.1044840

Levinas, Durkheim, and the Everyday Ethics of Education

ANNA STRHAN

Abstract

This article explores the influence of Émile Durkheim on the philosophy of Emmanuel Levinas in order both to open up the political significance of Levinas's thought and to develop more expansive meanings of moral and political community within education. Education was a central preoccupation for both thinkers: Durkheim saw secular education as the site for promoting the values of organic solidarity, while Levinas was throughout his professional life engaged in debates on Jewish education and conceptualized ethical subjectivity as a condition of being taught. Durkheim has been accused of dissolving the moral into the social, and his view of education as a means of imparting a sense of civic republican values is sometimes seen as conservative, while Levinas's argument for an 'unfounded foundation' for morality is sometimes seen as paralyzing the impetus for concrete political action. Against these interpretations, I argue that their approaches present provocative challenges for conceptualizing the nature of the social, offering theoretical resources to deepen understanding of education as the site of an everyday ethics and a prophetic politics opening onto more compelling ideals for education than those dominant within standard educational discourses.

In January, 2011, the UK education minister at the time, Michael Gove, launched a review of the national curriculum for primary and secondary schools in England, provoking unease from teachers. His draft proposals for a new history curriculum were especially controversial. The issue, as Bhambra (2013) notes, was the use of an 'Our Island Story' narrative. This recalls a history book for children written in 1905, examining British history only within the nation's geographical borders and neglecting the fact that at the time, the UK governed at least a quarter of the earth's land and over a fifth of its population. The resistance of schoolteachers and historians to these proposals reflects a moral awareness that the representation of our collective past in education is central to the politics of the present, as a narrow vision of history can be associated with exclusionary social policies. Bhambra notes that this parochial vision of British history was being formulated at the same time as migrants are being increasingly scapegoated in British political discourse, citing a statement by a Liberal Democrat MP from the General Election campaign of 2010:

> We're in danger of a lost generation—parents and grandparents worry about a future where their children can't repay student loans, can't find a decent job and don't have a sniff of a chance at getting on the housing ladder. Their concern about the knock-on effects of immigration is genuine and isn't racist. (cited in ibid.)

The suggestion in these words is that immigrants are the cause of these problems. What is not being said is that 'it was a British government that brought in tuition fees and undercut access to higher education; it was a British government that undermined the unions and deregulated the labor market; and it was a British government that sold off council houses, didn't build any more, and thus allowed the pool of social housing to contract' (Bhambra, 2013).

The political offensive against immigration can be seen as the thin end of a wedge undermining a cosmopolitan welcoming of plurality. Bhambra notes that prominent members of the Coalition government (the Justice Secretary, Chris Grayling, and the Home Secretary, Theresa May), for example, sought to challenge a central pillar of cosmopolitanism—the commitment to human rights demonstrated by participation in the European Court of Human Rights and the Human Rights Act—through lobbying for the UK to pull out of the court and the convention, in a move which members of their own party, such as the former justice secretary, Kenneth Clarke, described as undermining fundamental freedoms that are 'at the heart of the idea of European civilisation' (Bhambra, 2013).

This debate about how the teaching of history can be implicated in perpetuating an exclusionary politics raises fundamental moral questions about how we talk about and enact the meaning of community and society within education. Bhambra argues that while any political community has to express itself as a 'we', that 'we' can be imagined as including the 'waves of immigrants' attacked by the coalition government: this 'more expansive and inclusive "we" might also be conscious of the widening social and economic inequalities brought about by the abstractions of neoliberal policy. Our problem is not the disruption of the social fabric by immigrants and by the exercise of human rights, but the separation from common problems of a distant political class and their active denial of an inclusive public interest' (Bhambra, 2013).

How might we express and enact this more expansive 'we' within education? Much contemporary debate about education is framed in terms of economic utility, with questions about 'the good' evacuated from public discourse. Yet this debate demonstrates an ethical concern about the exclusionary effects of a narrow-minded narrative of British history and raises the importance of attending to the ways particular political and moral ideals are folded into the everyday language and contents of the curriculum. Reflection on the ethics of education has always been central to philosophy of education, but in the past decade, there has been a growing interest in 'the ethical' from across the humanities and social sciences, and in broader public discourse. There are good reasons for this. In privileging private individual success and

LEVINAS AND THE PHILOSOPHY OF EDUCATION

fulfillment, modern Western culture has shifted questions about what it means to live a good life out of public debate, so that within education, policy discussions are mostly framed around neoliberal logics of the marketplace, utility, competitiveness and efficiency. The financial crisis and subsequent years of economic scarcity have returned ethical questions to the forefront of public and academic agendas, forcing reflection on fundamental moral questions such as how seemingly scarce resources are to be allocated and what forms of justice we hope for in our lives together.

Specific attention to the ethical has been something of a blindspot in social scientific theorizing. This may seem surprising, given that the founding theorists of the social sciences were preoccupied with exploring the nature of moral facts and values. Anthropologists have argued that it was in part Durkheim's identification of the moral law with society that inhibited examination of the ethical dimensions of society in anthropology (Laidlaw, 2002; Zigon, 2007). At the same time, although Emmanuel Levinas's focus on ethics has influenced educational philosophy (e.g. Standish, 2007; Strhan, 2012; Todd, 2008) and other humanities disciplines, it has yet to fully permeate social scientific debates to deepen understanding of the ethical within everyday life.

This article speculates on Durkheim's influence on Levinas to open up reflection on how we understand the moral nature of social life and human subjectivity, and the political challenge of this. Most scholarship on Levinas has located his work too exclusively within the phenomenological tradition, and, as Howard Caygill argues,[1] the price has been a loss of the political significance of his work. Durkheim has been accused of dissolving the moral into the social, and his educational focus on imparting civic republican values is sometimes seen as conservative. Against such interpretations, I will argue that reading their work together offers resources for deepening understanding of how we conceptualize social life and of education as the site of ethics.

Levinas, Durkheim, and Republican Modernity

In his interviews with Philip Nemo, Levinas said of his education at Strasbourg that it was an 'initiation into the great philosophers', but that 'it was Durkheim and Bergson who seemed to me especially alive in the instruction and attention of the students. It was they whom one cited, and whom one opposed' (*EI*, p. 26). The university at that time was marked by the 'principles of '89'[2]—a radical republicanism, which meant that even in the most abstract philosophical analyses, attention to the relation between the principles of liberty, equality and fraternity were never far below the surface (Caygill, 2002, p. 7). This climate played an important part in determining Levinas's later engagements with phenomenology. Following the Dreyfus Affair,[3] debates on the relations between these revolutionary principles had taken on a new intensity, provoking arguments on the Republican ideals which were still reverberating when Levinas arrived at Strasbourg in 1923 (Caygill, 2002, p. 7). The Affair had a profound effect in shaping Levinas's politics, stimulating an ongoing desire to reinvigorate the secular trinity of French revolutionary values, especially in relation to fraternity.[4] This was necessary after the anti-Dreyfusard *Action Française* and the Catholic Church had defined fraternity in narrow terms of national, religious, and racial identifications: any new conceptualization had to protect against those excluded through such categorizations (p. 9). Rather than interpreting fraternity in its Jacobin formulation as an armed male nation, or through categories of identification such as race, class, or religion, Levinas was inspired by his teachers at Strasbourg to develop 'an ethical concept of fraternity framed in terms of solidarity with the victim of injustice' (p. 8).

As site of struggle for the meaning of French Republicanism, the Dreyfus Affair played an important role in Levinas's intellectual formation and had decisively shaped Durkheim's sociological and political trajectory. Prior to the Affair, Durkheim had been developing a critique of classical liberalism's assumptions that society is comprised of disparate individuals pursuing private concerns. At the height of the Affair, as people took to the streets, waving flags and expressing creeds, he perceived a shared faith in civic republicanism or 'moral individualism' being affirmed and deepened and saw this as affirming a faith that people do not live for themselves alone, but for others (Cladis, 2001, p. xv). In 'Individualism and the Intellectuals', Durkheim argued that the moral individualism associated with liberalism is inseparable from fraternity, or 'organic solidarity', which inspires a feeling of sacredness: 'whoever makes an attempt on a man's life, on a man's liberty ... inspires in us a feeling of horror analogous in every way to that which the believer experiences when he sees his idol profaned. Such an ethic ... is a religion in which man is at once the worshipper and the god (1973, p. 46).

Durkheim's conception of 'the social' was also to be a significant influence on Levinas. Levinas described the work of Durkheim as

> an elaboration of the fundamental categories of the social, ... beginning with the idea that the social does not reduce to the sum of individual psychologies. Durkheim, a metaphysician! The idea that the social is the very order of the spiritual, a new plot in being above the animal and human psychism; the level of 'collective representations' defined with vigor and which opens up the dimension of spirit in the individual life itself, where the individual alone comes to be recognized and even redeemed. In Durkheim there is, in a sense, a theory of 'levels of being,' of the irreducibility of these levels to one another. (*EI*, pp. 26–27)

For Levinas, Durkheim's understanding of the 'social' opened up ontological difference, revealing the irreducibility of modes of being to each other. Against the view of his reducing the moral to the social, Durkheim, for Levinas, revealed the social precisely *as* the site of transcendence, elevating the very meaning of 'society'. Levinas's desire to reconceptualize human subjectivity as beginning in ethical responsibility takes up elements of this moral orientation of Durkheim's work. Human life, for both, begins from the social fact of our being-*for*-others, and this determines the nature of subjectivity as ethical.

Durkheim's argument that, in Levinas's words, 'the social is the order of the spiritual', and that it is society that is venerated in religious rituals, is still, despite its familiarity, provocative. Society, Durkheim writes, 'arouses in us a sensation of perpetual dependence', and we feel society as both 'other' than but also working through us, as it 'compels us to become its servants, forgetting our own interests, and compels us to endure all sorts of hardships, privations, and sacrifice without which social life would be impossible' (2001, pp. 154–155). This sensation of society as sacred shapes human subjectivity as fundamentally dividual. Durkheim argues that in our social condition of obligation toward others, we feel a moral call as expressing 'something inside us other than ourselves' (pp. 193–194). Durkheim argued that with processes of modernization, as societies 'expand over vaster territories, traditions and practices' (1973, p. 51), only a sense of the dignity of the human could be a primary source of solidarity, emerging not from any sense of sameness of persons or categories of identity, but in the sacredness of humanity and the sense of solidarity for the other who is the victim of injustice.

Durkheim saw education as the sphere where this moral solidarity could be deepened, and his 1902 lectures on moral education articulated a vision of the ethical as permeating the whole of education: 'it is implicated in every moment. It must be mingled in the whole of school life, as morality itself is involved in the whole web of collective life ... There is no formula that can contain and express it adequately' (cited in Cladis, 1998, p. 21). Durkheim had in mind a new secular ethics of education, based on a sense of respect for the innate dignity of the human individual as the core value of modern society. While he saw the idea of the nation as important in citizenship education, the nation should also always to open to scrutiny, for example, in respect to the extent to which it promoted justice for those outside. The nation, for Durkheim, could enjoy moral primacy only on condition that its actions were constantly open to moral question, that it was not understood 'as an unscrupulous self-centered being, solely preoccupied with expansion and self-aggrandizement to the detriment of similar entities; but as one of many agencies that must collaborate for the progressive realization of the conception of mankind' (cited in Bellah, 1973, p. xli).

In this brief sketch, we see that rather than reducing the moral to the social, Durkheim elevates the social to the moral and develops a vision of modern societies as underpinned by a solidarity beginning not in conditions of sameness, but in recognition of the dignity of the other human, starting from compassion for the victim of injustice. How then do these ideas relate to Levinas's understanding of social life and to his thinking on education? In the following section, let us consider how these ideas find expression in Levinas's thought.

Justice, Society, and Prophetic Politics

Levinas's work is dominated by one far-reaching theme: that ethics is first philosophy. In *Difficult Freedom*, Levinas described his life as 'a disparate inventory ... dominated by the presentiment and memory of the Nazi horror' (*DF*, p. 291): his conceptualization of human subjectivity, language, and knowledge as beginning with ethics was determined by his experience of National Socialism, both feared and mourned.

LEVINAS AND THE PHILOSOPHY OF EDUCATION

Levinas's two major works—*Totality and Infinity* and *Otherwise than Being*—are works of mourning, reflected in the dedication of *Otherwise than Being*, in 'memory of those who were closest among the six million assassinated by the National Socialists, and of the millions on millions of all confessions and all nations, victims of the same hatred of the other man, the same anti-semitism'. The trajectory of Levinas's work was significantly shaped by his engagement with Heidegger. After Strasbourg, Levinas went to study with Husserl in Freiburg, but the approach he discovered in Husserl was, he stated, 'transfigured by Heidegger' (*RB*, p. 32).[5] Although his attraction to Heidegger's work was ended by Heidegger's commitment to National Socialism, this initial influence played a significant part in orientating the direction of Levinas's work, subsequently governed by 'the profound desire to leave the climate of that [Heidegger's] philosophy' (*EE*, p. 4).

The urgency of leaving Heideggerian philosophy is evident in Levinas's presentiments of the Nazi horror. His 'Reflections on the Philosophy of Hitlerism', published in 1934, described the Heideggerian ontology of the self as a precondition of National Socialism. Levinas described the article as motivated by the belief that 'the source of the bloody barbarism of National Socialism lies not in some contingent anomaly within human reasoning, nor in some accidental ideological misunderstanding' (*RPH*, p. 63). He summarized the article as identifying the source of '*elemental Evil* into which we can be led by logic and against which Western philosophy had not sufficiently insured itself' as 'inscribed within the ontology of a being concerned with being' (p. 63). In this early writing, we see already the future direction of Levinas's work in this idea that the self-positing subject, concerned with its own being, 'the famous subject of a transcendental idealism that before all else wishes to be free and thinks itself free' (p. 63), leads to the possibility of political violence.

This article reveals how Levinas's critique of Heidegger was influenced by Durkheim. As Caygill notes, Levinas's analysis of Hitlerism as an elaboration of an 'elementary form' of evil was informed by Durkheim's method of studying the 'elementary forms' of religion a means of understanding the sacred in more complex modernized societies (Caygill, 2002, p. 31). Here, Levinas brings this approach together with phenomenology to explore the 'elementary forms' and temporal structures of experience shaping Nazism and its oppositions in Christianity and liberalism. Levinas argues that in Nazism, as an 'elementary form' of pagan religion, the past is a fait accompli that weighs heavily on human destiny, as both present and future repeat a past that can only be endured (Caygill, 2002, p. 33). Levinas argues that true freedom requires a true present, offered by Jewish and Christian temporalities with their dramas of repentance and redemption, in which there is 'a continuous opening on to the future' (p. 33).

Responsibility is intrinsic to this understanding of freedom, and equality here is rooted in the liberatory potential of monotheism. Levinas's primary concern is to derive equality from freedom, in order to defend it from fascist conceptions of racial inequality. This, as Caygill notes, is a thread Levinas develops in later writings, using the notion of freedom both to criticize any notion of fate (whether rooted in racial philosophies of history or natural history) and then to justify equality. In absolute freedom, the individual is 'liberated ... from any determination be it natural (racial) or historical (political or confessional)' (Caygill, 2002, p. 34), so that the equal dignity of each human, as emphasized by Durkheim, is justified not through material or social conditions, but through 'the power given to the soul to free itself from *what has been*, from everything that linked it with something or engaged it with something' (*RPH*, p. 66).

Levinas criticizes liberalism as unable to protect the dignity of the human subject, since it depends on a self-positing, autonomous subject. As Durkheim had earlier challenged individualistic conceptions of liberalism through showing human subjectivity as shaped through a primary *moral* obligation, so Levinas questions whether liberalism 'is all we need' to 'achieve an authentic dignity for the human subject. Does the subject arrive at the human condition prior to assuming responsibility for the other man ... ?' (*RPH*, p. 63). Levinas describes liberalism as accepting a radical concept of freedom, with reason the source of freedom, located 'outside the brutal world and the implacable history of concrete existence' (p. 66). This reign of reason, beginning in the Enlightenment, displaces the redemptive time of Christianity, so that 'in place of liberation through grace, there is autonomy' (p. 66). Levinas argues that this autonomy, without a shared drama of repentance and redemption, fails to offer a basis for community or social life, making liberalism vulnerable to suggestions for 'community' or 'fraternity' opposed to freedom or equality, 'such as the national, confessional, class and, more ominously, racial fraternities that pervade modernity and are able through their own dramatic narratives of repentance and redemption to exploit the deficit of liberal rationalism' (Caygill, 2002, p. 35).

'Reflections on the Philosophy of Hitlerism' reveals how Levinas's approach was influenced by Durkheim from this early period. Developing this, in *Totality and Infinity*, Levinas's critique extends beyond Heidegger to interrogate the entire Western philosophical tradition. The terms 'totality' and 'infinity' draw a contrast between a totalizing ontological approach and an ethical relation of infinitude. Levinas's central argument is that if our relations with others are conceived in terms of comprehension, recognition, or equality, then insofar as this mode of relationality aims to bring the other within the domain of *my* understanding, it is totalizing. This idea of taking over the other, and the endless capacities of Western thought to do this, is central to Levinas's philosophy and has relevance beyond the horizons he identified. Robert Eaglestone notes that colonial projects have been based on this logic of 'annexation, of conquering, which means consuming otherness and revising it as "sameness"' (2010, p. 64). As today such exploitative modes of relationality continue by other means, Levinas's thought 'is a way of exposing, from within, the colonial and "omnivorous" powers of Western thought' (Eaglestone, 2010, p. 64). Today, this totalizing impulse can also be seen in dehumanizing discourses of accumulation, performativity, and productivity that pervade education, in which the singularity of the other is subsumed as they are measured according to their capacity for production.

Levinas describes the relation between self and other that interrupts this totalizing relation as taking place in language: the site of totality *and* infinity. Describing responsibility (as responsivity) as a precondition of language, Levinas anchors the structure of logical thought in this ethical relation to the other, even if this always carries with it the possibility of totalization. Levinas uses an image of a teacher to evoke this ethical relation between self and other: to be taught is to be summoned into a non-violent relation with the other, who remains beyond my knowing in a position of magisterial height: 'The height from which language comes we designate with the term teaching ... This voice coming from another shore teaches transcendence itself. Teaching signifies the whole infinity of exteriority' (*TI*, p. 271).

For Levinas, it is only in being taught that meaning, truth, and subjectivity are possible, and these come to me from beyond—even as they are within—myself and shape the conditions of my subjectivity as dividual, as Durkheim had earlier argued. Through this teaching, a common social world is created: 'To speak is to make the world common, to create commonplaces. Language does not refer to the generality of concepts, but lays the foundation for a possession in common' (*TI*, p. 76). This teaching founds objectivity and reason, which is the result of putting things in question between self and other. As Alphonso Lingis puts this:

> The other turns and speaks; he or she asks something of me. Her words, which I understand because they are the words of my own tongue, ask for information and indications. They ask for a response that will be responsible, will give reasons for its reasons and will be a commitment to answer for what it answers. But they first greet me with an appeal for responsiveness. (1994, pp. 130–131).

As for Durkheim, society and rationality are possible through a condition of moral obligation, Levinas likewise opens up the ethical conditions of subjectivity, society, and reason.

Levinas, however, deepens the nature of this responsibility. For Durkheim, it is possible to understand the subject's obligation toward others as what Stanley Cavell 'describes as a "horizontal form of life"' (1996). Cavell uses this phrase to allude to an interpretation of Wittgenstein's use of the phrase 'form of life' in a conventionalist sense, to refer to human beings agreeing with each other in the language they use, as 'some kind of contract or an implicitly or explicitly agreed upon set of rules' (Cavell, 1996, p. 328). For Durkheim, the subject's sense of moral obligation toward others might be seen in such terms, as a reciprocal responsibility, rooted in the experience of being part of a social collective. For Levinas, the ethical dividualism of the subject might be seen instead in terms of a 'vertical form of life' (Cavell, 1996, p. 328). In this, what is at issue are 'not alone differences between promising and fully intending, or between coronations and inaugurations, or between barter and a credit system...; these are differences within the plane, the horizon, of the social, of human society' (p. 329). While Levinas saw Durkheim's conception of 'the social' as opening up ontological difference, his own work deepens this, with subjectivity and society beginning not in a reciprocal form of life, but in the verticality of human responsibility.

Cavell suggests that our becoming disappointed with criteria, indeed with language as such, is a consequence of this vertical form of life, of the singularity and separateness of *my* experience, which is the condition of human subjectivity: 'not a particular fact or power but the fact that I am a man, therefore of *this* (range or scale of) capacity for work, for pleasure, for endurance, for appeal, for command, for understanding, for wish, for will, for teaching, for suffering' (p. 330). For Levinas, it is the responsibility of subjectivity that confirms the singularity of the subject, and the vertiginous height of this orientation toward the other interrupts and leaves us disappointed with categories of identification. This takes us somewhat beyond Durkheim's organic solidarity. Levinas emphasizes that this inescapable responsibility deepens the more I choose to answer it, and while I may ignore it, I cannot escape the call by which I am singularly addressed: 'To utter "I", to affirm the irreducible singularity in which the apology is pursued, means to possess a privileged place with regard to responsibilities for which no one can replace me and from which no one can release me' (*TI*, p. 245).

Although Levinas focuses on the relationship between I and other to draw attention to the nature of singularity (the responsibility that begins in *me*, that confirms *my* uniqueness), within everyday social life, this is not a party of two. The third party is always present in the other's address, demanding justice and justification for how I respond to many others. The ethical is therefore always already inseparable from the political, as the third interrupts the asymmetry of responsibility, demanding justice (*TI*, p. 213). Levinas develops this line of thought in *Otherwise than Being*, with society founded not on equality or commonality, but on a community of others, each unique and resisting reduction to classification. This deepens Durkheim's understanding of the social as founded in the experience of obligation for others, but resisting Durkheim's emphasis on fusion in the ecstatic moment of worship. Levinas's emphasis on the singularity and separateness of the subject indexes the unknowability of the other, allowing a more expansive understanding of community and society beginning in this fundamental condition of difference and *ethical* responsibility for the other.

Levinas posits this notion of justice associated with the third as maintaining the self's infinite responsibility, but balanced against working out the conditions of justice for all the others. Caygill argues that this position is limited: Levinas ends up unexpectedly insisting on the priority of the relation to the other over the third, to prevent the other's absorption into the totality (Caygill, 2002, p. 142), leaving the possibility of violence against the third party in the name of the other. Caygill however considers the possibility of the reverse of this position, in which all thirds become others, and suggests that this more compelling vision for justice is provided through the concepts of fraternity and illeity (p. 143).

Levinas uses the concept 'illeity' to signify 'the Infinite that escapes the objectification of thematization and of dialogue ... in the third person' (*OB*, p. 150). Illeity is not only a third between self and neighbor, but a third between immanence and transcendence that hollows out the distance between self and neighbor while always exceeding the terms of any relation (Caygill, 2002, p. 147; Strhan, 2012, p. 154). With illeity, Levinas refuses Durkheimian fusion and deepens the ethical possibilities of subjectivity through instead emphasizing the space of separation between self and other. In a dense passage, Levinas describes how the self finds within itself the infinite demand addressed to me by the other, in having already been obedient to their order:

LEVINAS AND THE PHILOSOPHY OF EDUCATION

> The inscription of the order in the for-the-other of obedience is an anarchic being affected, which slips into me 'like a thief' through the outstretched nets of consciousness. This trauma has surprised me completely; the order has never been presented ... to the point that it is I that only says, and after the event, this unheard-of obligation. This ambivalence is the exception and subjectivity of the subject, its very psyche, a possibility of inspiration. It is the possibility of being the author of what had been breathed in unbeknownst to me, of having received, one knows not from where, that of which I am author. In the responsibility for the other we are at the heart of the ambiguity of inspiration. The unheard-of saying is enigmatically in the anarchic response, in my responsibility for the other. The trace of infinity is this ambiguity in the subject, in turns beginning and makeshift, a diachronic ambivalence which ethics makes possible. (*OB*, pp. 148–149)

Caygill suggests that this voice heard in the command might be the voice of the third, overturning the priority of the other. This gestures toward a 'prophetic politics', rooted in fraternity:

> Prophetic politics opens the possibility for a notion of justice as perpetual interruption, of the self by the other and of the other by the third. The third in question here, and the justice to which it gives rise, is not the third of the state and its justice thought of in terms of equivalence and measure, but the third thought of in terms of divinity and in the divine approbation of human fraternity. (Caygill, 2002, p. 150)

Levinas describes the other as also my brother, and states that it is impossible to deny fraternity (*OB*, p. 150), suggesting a prophetic understanding of community beginning with the condition of fraternity conceived in terms of responsibility, rather than sameness or fusion. This fraternity is bound up with the separation of illeity: 'It is not because the neighbor would be recognized as belonging to the same genus as me that he concerns me. He is precisely *other*. The community with him begins in my obligation to him ... A fraternity that cannot be abrogated, an unimpeachable assignation' (p. 87).

For Levinas, this responsibility to the other and all the others is found first of all in my condition of being taught by the other, through whom I receive language and the uniqueness of my subjectivity. This responsibility, deepening the more I attend to it, is always there, and Levinas prophetically invites his reader to attend to it, to bring about a more just society, rooted in responsibility for *all* the others, in which my obligations to those close by are structured by my relations to all the others.

Durkheim's focus on the ritualization of the sacred emphasizes the experiential qualities through which moral sensibilities are inculcated, yet Levinas draws this intuition into the realm of the everyday: this is not a matter of peak experiences, or of 'experience' at all, but a condition of responsibility that is present as a possibility to be realized in every interaction. As Standish questions, what do we do 'that does *not* involve this responsibility—neglected or covered over though that usually is. If the obligation to the Other should be seen as pervasive, the things that we interact with and the way we word the world should be seen in this light (2007, pp. 79–80). Although this responsibility extends to our responsibilities for *all*, it is there in the most mundane of interactions, 'even the simple, "After you, sir" ... [This is] not the limit case of solidarity, but the condition for all solidarity' (*OB*, p. 117). For Levinas, society depends not on any notion of truth or knowledge, but on this. Criticizing the Platonic subordination of justice to truth, he argues, 'Society does not proceed from the contemplation of the true; truth is made possible by relation with the Other ... Truth is thus bound up with the social relation, which is justice' (*TI*, p. 72).

As Durkheim was engaged in debates about French education, so Levinas spent most of his professional life as a school administrator and teacher. From 1945–1979, Levinas was Director of the École Normale Israélite Orientale, a work he described as 'a calling', in a school training teachers to work in the Mediterranean region, working 'for the emancipation of Jews in those countries where they still did not have the right to citizenship' (*RB*, p. 38). Although sometimes criticized as relegating ethics to an otherworldly order, Levinas's conception of responsibility as working for an always better justice was something he was concretely working out in his own life in the domain of education. His comments on the pedagogical demands he experienced at the ENIO can be connected with his conceptualization of subjectivity as a deepening responsibility:

> Will my life have been spent between the incessant presentiment of Hitlerism and the Hitlerism that refuses itself to any forgetting? Not everything related in my thoughts to the destiny of Judaism, but my activity at the Alliance kept me in contact with the Jewish ordeal, bringing me back to the concrete social and political problems which concerned it everywhere. In Europe, outside of the Mediterranean region of the schools of the Alliance: notably in Poland, where the proximity of a hostile Germany nevertheless remained anti-Semitic instincts barely put to sleep. Concrete problems with spiritual repercussions. Facts that are always enormous. Thoughts coming back to ancient and venerable texts, always enigmatic, always disproportionate to the exegeses of a school. Here you have, in administrative and pedagogical problems, invitations to a deepening, to a becoming conscience, that is, to Scripture. (*RB*, p. 39)

However, although this deepening responsibility invites concrete action to work toward a better justice, this does not mean that any programmatic application of his thought to education follows (Todd, 2008, p. 182). While Durkheim developed an approach to moral education for schools to deepen social solidarity, Levinas leaves radically open the question of *how* to deepen the ethical possibilities that are already implied in our everyday educational worlds.

Discussion: Toward an Everyday Ethics of Education

Reading Levinas with Durkheim shows the extent to which Levinas was concerned with taking up the challenge he had encountered in Durkheim's thought to revitalize political principles. It also invites us to reconsider Durkheim's metaphysics of the social, in which the social is elevated to the transcendent rather than the moral dissolved into the social. There are significant differences between their approaches, most pointedly in relation to the singularity of subjectivity. Yet their conceptions of education—rooted in a sense of social life as beginning with ethics—demonstrates the narrowness of totalizing educational discourses in which, for example, education is treated as a service that can be delivered to consumers in an educational marketplace, a domain of increasingly conceived in terms of privatized choice rather than public good.

There are limitations to their approaches. Durkheim's patriotism sounds a paternalistic note, and his duality of sacred and profane and desire to create a moral community always run the risk of exclusion. The contemporary resonance of this was powerfully suggested in responses to the attack on the French magazine *Charlie Hebdo* in January, 2015, as the sacralizing of 'free speech' symbolized in the 'Je Suis Charlie' slogans reverberating on social media and on demonstrators' placards were experienced by many as perpetuating an exclusionary logic against those unable to express solidarity with the satirical magazine.[6] Levinas's own political refusals of responsibility and justice are also well documented (Strhan, 2012, p. 164). But these risks of exclusion and totalization should invite our attention to *our* own need for vigilance against becoming immunized against others' needs and to work to resist deafness to the address of those both within and beyond our communities. Responsibility is to those nearby. But it is also for those far away who are affected by our actions in an increasingly globalized world, and the notions of 'I' and 'we' that we voice within education might enable a more expansive political imaginary and deepen desire for educational communities that are bound together with an orientation of responsibility toward those within and beyond them, a desire to welcome and to protect the other that challenges the exclusionary logics that are today increasingly sounding again, as far-right political parties grow in prominence across Europe and elsewhere.

Levinas shows us how the resources for a more ethical thinking are already present in our engagements with others in education, and shows us that dehumanizing logics of productivity or historical narratives perpetuating an exclusionary political vision of 'community' are never the whole story. Students and teachers in responding to each other with responses that *are* responsible, or in the curriculum choices they make about which stories they tell about the possibilities of a more just society, are already showing how our practices and words can bear witness to an everyday ethics that *is* also achieved, even if that achievement is also always fragile, threatened by the risk of refusal to acknowledge some part of the community (e.g. minority groups) as an integral part of it.

Levinas and Durkheim both invite us to be more attentive to the moral possibilities that are already implied in everyday educational practices, inviting a prophetic politics of radical inclusion. Their commitments to the human and to education as fundamentally moral are imbued with a hopefulness in the possibility of change. Vaclav Havel describes how he was influenced by Levinas's notion of responsibility, this idea that 'something must begin', that we should have greater faith in the potential significance of our everyday actions:

LEVINAS AND THE PHILOSOPHY OF EDUCATION

> You have certainly heard of the 'butterfly effect'. It is a belief that everything in the world is so mysteriously and completely interconnected that a slight, seemingly insignificant wave of a butterfly's wings in a single spot on this planet can unleash a typhoon thousands of miles away.
>
> I think we must believe in this effect for politics. We cannot assume that our microscopic yet truly unique everyday actions are of no consequence simply because they cannot resolve the immense problems of today. That would be an a priori nihilistic assertion, and an expression of the arrogant, modern rationality that believes it knows how the world works. (cited in Edgoose, 2008, p. 111)

Levinas and Durkheim encourage us to attend to the everyday moral landscapes of education that we exist within, and to be aware that it is through our actions that such landscapes are re-created. We may *feel* subjected to social forces beyond our control, but that social realm is *also* shaped and made possible through our words and responses to each other. We *can* hope that our actions and words matter in the work of creating a better justice. We *can* find ways of resisting unjust words, practices, and the colonization of our thinking about education in totalizing rhetorics, whether in dehumanizing logics of efficiency, or in terms of social exclusion. Our actions and the words we speak, as teachers and students, have a political and ethical power that exceeds our intentions or knowledge, and Levinas and Durkheim witness to that fact, encouraging us to be vigilant that our educational practices enact a more humane society.

Abbreviations

DF	Difficult Freedom
EI	Ethics and Infinity
OB	Otherwise than Being
RB	Is It Righteous to Be?
RPH	Reflections on the Philosophy of Hitlerism
TI	Totality and Infinity

Acknowledgements

I am grateful to the Leverhulme Trust for funding, through the Early Career Fellowship Scheme. A version of this article was presented at the UCL Institute of Education, Philosophy of Education Research Seminar. I would like to thank Ruth Sheldon, Guoping Zhao, and the two anonymous reviewers for their comments on an earlier draft.

Disclosure statement

No potential conflict of interest was reported by the author.

Funding

This work was supported by the Leverhulme Trust [ECF-2012-605].

Notes

1. My interpretation of the relation between Levinas and Durkheim throughout this article is significantly influenced by Caygill's brilliant *Levinas and the Political* (2002).
2. These principles refer to the tradition of radical republicanism bequeathed by the French Revolution of 1789 (Caygill, 2002, p. 7).
3. This refers to the public upheaval over the case of Captain Alfred Dreyfus, a Jewish French military officer who was unjustly convicted of treason by a military tribunal and imprisoned on Devil's Island in French Guiana, where he spent five years. By 1898, the case had become a famous public affair, and many believed France's future as a democracy rested on the acquittal of Captain Dreyfus.
4. The term 'fraternity' is vulnerable to critique as a patriarchal idiom, however, as I will elaborate, Levinas's use of the term gestures more toward ideas of political friendship and community beginning in my responsibility, rather than necessarily signifying ideas of patriarchy.
5. See Strhan (2012, pp. 4–20).
6. See, for example, discussion in https://www.opendemocracy.net/can-europe-make-it/cas-mudde/no-we-are-not-all-charlie-and-that%E2%80%99s-problem (accessed 16 February 2015).

References

Bellah, R. (1973). Introduction. In E. Durkheim, *On morality and society: Selected writings* (pp. ix–lx). Chicago, IL: University of Chicago Press.

Bhambra, G. K. (2013). The dangerous politics of belonging. *Discover Society*, 1. Retrieved October 1, 2013, from http://www.discoversociety.org/the-dangerous-politics-of-belonging-a-grubby-island-story/

Cavell, S. (1996). Declining decline. In S. Mulhall (Ed.), *The Cavell reader* (pp. 321–352). Cambridge, MA: Blackwell.

Caygill, H. (2002). *Levinas and the political*. London: Routledge.

Cladis, M. S. (1998). Emile Durkheim and moral education in a pluralistic society. In G. Walford & W. S. F. Pickering (Eds.), *Durkheim and modern education* (pp. 19–45). London: Routledge.

Cladis, M. S. (2001). Introduction. In E. Durkheim, *The elementary forms of the religious life* (pp. vii–xxxvii). Oxford: Oxford University Press.

Durkheim, E. (1973). *On morality and society: Selected writings*. Chicago, IL: University of Chicago Press.

Durkheim, E. (2001). *The elementary forms of the religious life* (C. Cosman, Trans.). Oxford: Oxford University Press.

Eaglestone, R. (2010). Postcolonial thought and Levinas's double vision. In P. Atterton & M. Calarco (Eds.), *Radicalizing Levinas* (pp. 57–68). Albany: State University of New York Press.

Edgoose, J. (2008). Teaching our way out when nobody knows the way. In D. Égea-Kuehne (Ed.), *Levinas and education: At the intersection of faith and reason* (pp. 100–114). London: Routledge.

Laidlaw, J. (2002). For an anthropology of ethics and freedom. *Journal of the Royal Anthropological Institute, 8*, 311–332.

Levinas, E. (1969). *Totality and infinity* (A. Lingis, Trans.). Pittsburgh, PA: Duquesne University Press.

Levinas, E. (1981). *Otherwise than being* (A. Lingis, Trans.). The Hague: Martinus Nijhoff.

Levinas, E. (1985). *Ethics and infinity* (R. A. Cohen, Trans.). Pittsburgh, PA: Duquesne University Press.

Levinas, E. (1990a). *Difficult freedom* (S. Hand, Trans.). London: Athlone.

Levinas, E. (1990b). Reflections on the philosophy of Hitlerism. *Critical Inquiry, 17*, 63–71.

Levinas, E. (2001). In J. Robbins (Ed.), *Is it righteous to be?* Stanford, CA: Stanford University Press.

Lingis, A. (1994). *The community of those who have nothing in common*. Bloomington: Indiana University Press.

Standish, P. (2007). Education for grown-ups, a religion for adults: Scepticism and alterity in Cavell and Levinas. *Ethics and Education, 2*, 73–91.

Strhan, A. (2012). *Levinas, subjectivity, education: Towards an ethics of radical responsibility.* Chichester: Wiley-Blackwell.

Todd, S. (2008). Welcoming and difficult learning: Reading Levinas with education. In D. Égea-Kuehne (Ed.), *Levinas and education: At the intersection of faith and reason* (pp. 170–185). London: Routledge.

Zigon, J. (2007). Moral breakdown and the ethical demand: A theoretical framework for an anthropology of moralities. *Anthropological Theory, 7*, 131–150.

Singularity and Community: Levinas and democracy

Guoping Zhao

Abstract

This article explores and extends Levinas's ideas of singularity and community as multiplicity and argues that his identification of language and discourse as the means to create ethical communities provides tangible possibilities for rebuilding genuine democracy in a humane world. These ideas help us reimagine school and classroom as communities open to differences. They also give education the opportunity to support the emergence of the singular and the irreducible—infinite human beings.

Introduction

The idea of 'community' has recently been seriously examined and reformulated in the context of the anti-totalitarian movement of continental philosophy. Such interest in the idea of community is also situated in the broader social and political context of renewed interest in the long-lasting ideal of cosmopolitanism and recurrent inquiry into the meaning of democracy. Levinas's idea of singularity and multiplicity is part of the reformulation that emphasizes the irreducible subjectivity of singular individuals and the ethical relationships among them. However, while Levinas's ideas are eminently relevant and helpful, his 'tightly constrained systems of meaning' (Todd, this issue) and highly phenomenologically based descriptions often make their practical application difficult. In particular, Levinas locates the origin of ethical responsibility and human subjectivity itself in pre-ego and pre-conscious human existential experiences (Zhao, 2012); thus, the ideas of responsibility and subjectivity are rather novel within the Western tradition and pose daunting challenges in concrete political and educational settings. In this article, in an effort to engage Levinas with pressing socio-political and educational issues, I explore the trajectory of Levinas's thought, extending and drawing clear meanings and logical implications from his ideas to address questions of community in democracy and in education. I argue that his identification of language and discourse as the means to create ethical communities provides tangible possibilities for rebuilding genuine democracy in a human world. They also help us reimagine school and classroom communities that are open to differences and allow for the emerging of singular and irreducible human beings.

Recent Philosophical Developments in the Idea of Community and Education

In the past two decades, European continental philosophy has increasingly concerned itself with social and political matters (Elliott, 2009), and as a result, examining and rearticulating the idea of community has become central to some of its key thinkers, including Maurice Blanchot, Emmanuel Levinas, Jacques Derrida, Jean-Luc Nancy, and Giorgio Agamben. In the West, the idea of community has traditionally been construed as a communion, as the coming together of a group of people who share something in common: language, belief, culture, and identity. Community, the knowing and harmonizing of the group members, gives the members a sense of safety and comfort and guards them from the difference of the other. Such a notion of community, particularly when applied to social and political arenas, is now considered dangerous and consequently has been challenged and deconstructed by most of these thinkers. Derrida in particular reminds us that the word 'community' means a kind of 'military formation', a wall of protection that we build against the other (Caputo, 1997, pp. 271–272). May (1997) explains: 'Thinking of community in terms of a common substance that we all must participate in marginalizes those who are different from the participants' (p. 4). It is part of the totalitarian thinking of modern philosophy, which 'eliminates that which is different' (ibid.); as philosophical thinking, its 'links with political totalitarianism are not far to seek' (ibid.). Nazism in Germany and fascism in Italy, for instance, are widely acknowledged political totalitarianisms based on such thinking. In contemporary social and political lives, racism, sexism, heterosexism, and religious fundamentalism are also manifestations of such totalitarian thinking, where one common substance/culture/identity is valorized at the expense of others.

The post-WWII philosophical movement of anti-totalitarianism calls for a different way of thinking and living 'that does not reduce others who may be unlike us to the status of mere things' (May, 1997, p. 9), and for this reason, the idea of community has been closely examined and reformulated. In continental philosophy, this reformulation has produced one noticeable trend, as shared by Blanchot, Derrida, and Nancy—caution about and questioning of the possibility or even the very idea of community. Nancy and Derrida, for example, question whether a positive articulation of community is possible and whether it necessarily leads to a totalitarian approach to community itself. Recognizing the need to write about and to cross out community at the same time, they suggest that we must put community constantly under erasure. Thus, Derrida proposes a 'community without community' (Derrida, 1997, p. 202) and Nancy proposes an 'inoperative community' (1991) which is 'at once the trace which will have made possible the existence of the social as such, and that which will have withdrawn or been denied in order that community may be' (Gaon, 2005, p. 395).

LEVINAS AND THE PHILOSOPHY OF EDUCATION

Against this common trend, however, Levinas does not shy away from a positive approach to community; and in fact, his community is conceived precisely in order to interrupt and break out of totality, to ensure a world where human subjectivity and alterity are received and respected without truncation. His *Totality and Infinity* (1969) can be read as outlining a human community in which the primacy of the infinite otherness of the other enacts an ethical relation among multiplicities. In the following sections, I explore in depth, and draw clear implications from, his articulation of singularity and multiplicity. Extending his ideas of language and discourse, I explicate how our social and political life—as well as education—can be transformed by these ideas.

The philosophical reformulation of the idea of community, particularly that of Levinas, has had a great impact on the thinking of educational theorists in recent years. Todd (2004), for example, articulates a notion of community in education 'as a signifying encounter with difference' (p. 337). Biesta (2004), differentiating two types of community, the 'rational community' and the 'community of those who have nothing in common', articulate the community that 'education and educators should be concerned with' (p. 307). Biesta's typology of community draws heavily on Alphonso Lingis's work, which is built upon Levinas's. The so-called rational community can be found in Habermas's communicative theory and Freire's dialogical pedagogy. According to Lingis and Biesta, while the rational community enables individuals to 'speak as "rational agents"' and ensures equity among individuals with differences, it is governed by 'a common language and a common logic' (p. 315) and is still based on a notion of essentially identifiable and interchangeable human subjects. The individual is a representative and a 'spokesperson' (p. 311), and different perspectives are taken as fully understandable and sharable. Visions and insights are depersonalized and there is no concern for individuality, singularity, and otherness. For Biesta, such a notion of community still compromises the otherness of the other and cannot be a viable educational community.

The 'community of those who have nothing in common', on the other hand, 'is the community in which we are all strangers for each other' (Biesta, 2004, p. 307). Drawing mostly on Levinas, Biesta emphasizes the 'ethical nature' (p. 318) of the community. In such a community, we 'speak in our own, unique, and unprecedented way … and we come into the world as unique and singular beings' (p. 315) in our response to the other. Ultimately, Biesta argues, educators should strive for such a community at school. Additionally, Chinnery (2007), 'pick[ing] up where Biesta leaves off', argues that 'the preconditions or moral dispositions' of such a 'community without identity … [are] compassion, … a particular kind of suffering-with-the-other' (p. 331).

While educational theorists have been deeply influenced by Levinas's notions of otherness and responsibility, I argue that Levinas's idea of community has not been fully explored and illuminated. It is still unclear how such a community is able to break through totality while maintaining an ethical bond among all members. How is the subjectivity and alterity of each member received and respected in this community, or how can community become a signifying 'encounter with difference' (Todd, 2004, p. 337)? In the next sections, I explicate, through a close reading of Levinas's

Totality and Infinity, his idea of community, the nature and characteristics of the community, and the relation among the multiplicities that has to be established for such a community to break out of totality.

Levinas's Singularity and Multiplicity

Levinas elaborates his idea of community—characterized by its irreducible multiplicity and plurality—in several places in *Totality and Infinity*. He starts by saying that genuine multiplicity cannot be viewed from an 'exterior point of view' (1969, p. 120). The 'ultimate reality' of the relation 'that unites [the individuals] into a multiplicity ... is not visible from the outside' (p. 120). The reason for the opacity of the relation in a community is that, according to Levinas, if it were captured from the outside, 'the multiplicity would form a totality' (p. 120). What this means is that the relation cannot be in the form of numbers, concepts, categories, or genera. The individuals in a community cannot be numerically connected identical samples, or individuations of a concept (a member of a culture, a party, etc.), or embodiments of a category (a race, a class, etc.), because if they were, from the outside, the community would become identifiable and totalizable by the very number, concepts, or categories. The community of common substances, therefore, in Levinas's view, is the community of totality.

To maintain genuine multiplicity, then, (1) individuals have to be considered singularly unique and different from each other, since they are not related by concepts, orders, or categories, and (2) the relation among individuals, from the I to the other, has to be a radically different kind, beyond any general form of relations. Thus, already implied in this notion of multiplicity is a notion of individual singularity. 'Pluralism implies a radical alterity of the other' (1969, p. 121), as Levinas claims. The radical alterity of the other ensures that the individual has a sense of opacity or 'secrecy' (p. 120) that cannot be penetrated by knowledge. The individual is the 'free being' (p. 73), free from conception, manifestation, and reduction. In pronouncing the radical alterity of the other, Levinas seems to have also implied a notion of irreducible subjectivity, which makes the radical alterity of the other possible. As Levinas explains, 'The I [as ipseity] is ... the mode in which the break-up of totality, which leads to the presence of the absolutely other, is concretely accomplished' (p. 118). Elsewhere (Zhao, in press) I have further elaborated a Levinasian subject, also drawing more broadly from the philosophy of difference (Nancy, Derrida), a posthumanist notion of subjectivity that is characterized both by its originality and inexhaustible multiplicity and by its sociality and responsibility, a singular subjectivity that cannot be totalized and replicated and that is alterior to any other.

Therefore, Levinas's notion of community is tied to a notion of irreducible subjectivity (or vice versa) that is singular with internal multiplicity, 'refractory to every typology, to every genus, to every characterology, to every classification' (Levinas, 1969, p. 73). Only these 'free beings' can produce a community of genuine multiplicity.

Also implied in Levinas's notion of community is a relation among individuals as radically different from all general relations, 'a relation without relation' (Blanchot,

1993, p. 73), a relation of absolute separation (rather than fusion and assimilation). 'In order that multiplicity be maintained, the relation proceeding from me to the Other—the attitude of one person with regard to another—must be stronger than the formal signification of conjunction' (Levinas, 1969, pp. 121–122). To maintain a community of irreducible singularities, then, the relation has to be first of all a relation where the uniqueness of individuals, their subjectivity and alterity, are maintained, received, and respected without truncation. Since the Other is the 'infinity', 'infinitely transcendent, infinitely foreign' (p. 194), and infinitely beyond my egoism and my grasp, it is also an ethical relation. May (1997) explains,

> For Levinas, the experience of the other, and specifically of the other as irreducible to my own experience, is the ethical experience par excellence. It is the confrontation with what resists the imposition of my own categories, and thus my own conceptual control. The fundamental ethical decision everyone must confront is whether to recognize and come to terms with this experience, ... or instead to refuse this experience and try to force the other into one's own categories, a project that Levinas calls 'totality'. (pp. 90–91)

Thus, the otherness of the other beckons me 'toward an I-can-not-know-what of the other' (May, 1997, p. 92). This refusing to impose, to overcome the other, and the respect, the unconditional receiving of the irreducible alterity of the other, instantiate an ethical relation and form the foundation of genuine multiplicity.

Levinas further argues that the strangeness of the other is at the same time the face of destitution, hunger, which calls for our responsibility and love. According to Levinas, the freedom of the other

> is also strangeness—destitution. ... To recognize the Other is to recognize a hunger. To recognize the Other is to give. But it is to give to the master, to the lord, to him whom one approaches as 'You' in a dimension of height. (Levinas, 1969, p. 75)

As human beings, we are responsible for receiving the others as they are, without reducing and imposition, but we are also responsible for others' destitution. We cannot watch others suffer or die without moral pangs and a sense of guilt. If we do nothing in the face of others' suffering, we are accomplices to their suffering. Levinas insists that this responsibility is not pity, nor generosity, and does not come from my rational decision or principle, but is a moral call of the highest order, absolute, unconditional, and sacred. For Levinas, our capability for such responsibility is the phenomenological basis for holiness, love, and sociality in a human world. Thus, in a community of singularities, the relation among individuals is my responsibility to the other, to receive and maintain his otherness and to alleviate his suffering and destitution; and my responsibility to every other is unique in its concrete 'straightforwardness' and 'sincerity' (p. 202), which will not be captured by rules and principles.

With such a notion of subjectivity as singularity and of community as ethical multiplicity, however, questions, particularly *practical* ones, remain: how are the radical alterity and subjectivity of individuals maintained, received, and respected without truncation in a community? How can such a community of singularity be signified? How can a relation 'without relation' and a relation of absolute separation be realized?

Relating Singularities—Language and Discourse

In Levinas's account, the only way to maintain the absolute separation between the self and the other where the alterity of the other is preserved and genuine plurality is produced is through language and discourse. Levinas says, 'The relationship of language implies transcendence, radical separation, the strangeness of the interlocutors, the revelation of the other to me. ... Discourse is thus the experience of something absolutely foreign, a *pure* "knowledge" or "experience"' (p. 73, emphasis in the original). Consequently, 'Absolute difference, ... is established only by language' (p. 195). 'Discourse is ... an original relation with exterior being' (p. 66), and 'Language presupposes ... a plurality' (p. 73).

According to Levinas, language and discourse have two functions: the expressive and the presentational. Language presents the common, 'convey[s] concepts, understanding, and thematizations, but language first of all is an address' (p. 73). Discourse relates to comprehension, but it relates first of all to 'what remains essentially transcendent' (p. 195). There are reason, logic, and presentation in language, but this function of language is situated in and made possible through language as expression, calls and responses between the self and others. Levinas argues that when we transmit meanings and ideas, 'I do not transmit to the Other what is objective for me: the objective becomes objective only through communication. ... What I communicate ... is already constituted in the function of others' (p. 210). 'To thematize is to offer the world to the Other in speech. ... The basis of objectivity is constituted in a purely subjective process' (pp. 209–210). Knowledge is possible only through, and as a function of, my expression to the other.

Consequently, language is first of all an expression among singularities, and 'in its expressive function language precisely maintains the other' (Levinas, 1969, p. 73). Anna Strhan (this issue) notes that for Levinas, language 'is the site of *both* totality and infinity' (emphasis in the original), but infinity preconditions and interrupts totality. Though presentation and conceptualization tend to reduce and objectify the other, their power is undermined already in language as expression. 'The knowledge that absorbs the Other is forthwith situated within the discourse I address to him' (Levinas, 1969, p. 195). Accordingly, a language-bond community cannot reduce the other into an object—'language institutes a relation irreducible to the subject-object relation' (p. 73).

Levinas's use of language apparently comes from the understanding of language as a separation between the signifier and the signified. Since language never directly corresponds with the thing or the concept it signifies, language can be seen as being forged out of difference and separation. With this understanding of language, therefore, the one we address and call upon through language is never '*expressed* ... [nor] *present*, does not attend his own manifestation, but is simply signified in it by a sign in a system of signs' (Levinas, 1969, p. 178, emphasis in the original). In language, 'a being ... is manifested precisely as absent from his manifestation: a manifestation in the absence of being' (p. 178).

May (1997) adds, 'This absence, this nonphenomenon, is not a lack but rather an irreducibility to presence. It reveals itself—as this absence—in the face of the other' (p. 92). Language can never capture or exhaust the other, but instead, it signifies and maintains the infinite otherness of the other. It is indeed the 'original relation' with the infinite other, as an expression, a speech, and a call. The link between expression and responsibility is 'the ethical condition or essence of language' (p. 200), Levinas claims.

Essentially, Levinas is offering an account of a humane, ethical community and society within which the Habermasian rational, communicative, discourse is situated. For Levinas and Habermas, language is the ultimate human relation, so they are both advocating a sort of communicative democracy, but Habermas's democracy is purely reason-based. Language is only the carrier of meaning, understanding, and reasoning. For Levinas, on the other hand, language is first and foremost an expression among humans, an expression that ultimately maintains the other's subjectivity, singularity, and alterity. Human relations have to be above all relations in which all are irreducibly received and addressed and become responsible to each other.

The expressive use of language, therefore, is essential in building a community of singularities. In the following, I explore the expressive function of language in human relations, particularly in the forms of attentive speaking and good listening. I argue that speaking and listening provide the prime occasions in which the radical relation among singularities is realized and our responsibility to each other is carried out.

Speaking and Listening: Cultivating a Community of Singularities

Levinas has discussed speech and speaking extensively in his work, providing important insights, but he has rarely touched on listening as part of the expressive use of language and discourse. In this section, I draw on Levinas, Alphonso Lingis (whose work is heavily influenced by Levinas) and the recent philosophy of listening in education to explore how speaking and listening can facilitate the receiving and respecting of others' subjectivity and alterity.

Speaking

In the Western philosophical tradition, the study of discourse has focused largely on the logos, the content, the arguments, and the perspectives of participants, as shown in Habermas's communicative theory. Departing from this tradition, Levinas distinguishes 'saying' from 'said' and uses their correlation to 'delineate the subject-object structure' (1969, p. 46). For Levinas, 'said' is the fixed form, the thematized, and the 'temporalization of essence', but 'saying' signifies the 'otherwise than being', that which cannot be 'exhausted in [its] manifestation' (p. 46). The speaking aspect of communication, or the saying, signifies the irreducibility of the speaker's subjectivity.

'Saying' signifies a trace to something that cannot be captured in 'said', much like what Hegel describes in *The Science of Logic* as the 'activity of thought' and its relation to 'content'. Hegel suggests that while the activity of thought, which is at work in all our ideas, purposes, interests and actions, is ... unconsciously busy ..., what we consciously attend to is the contents, the objects of our ideas, that in which we are interested; on this basis, the determinations of thought have the significance of forms which are only attached to the content, but are not the content itself. (Hegel, 2001, p. 8)

Saying and thinking involve much more than what we consciously attend to, the content or the said, and include the unfathomable, pre-ego, pre-conscious activities and experiences. 'Speech proceeds from absolute difference' (Levinas, 1969, p. 194), or from the 'absence' that cannot be reduced to presence.

Thus, the 'said' is that which is thematized, 'temporalized', or objectified, but the 'saying' is the activity, the occasion where the speaker's subjectivity, in its inexhaustibility and originality, is signified. 'To present oneself by signifying is to speak', Levinas maintains (p. 66). Such signification calls the other, addresses him/her; it is a call to the other that the other cannot evade. The expression, speaking, 'surmounts and ... calls me to responsibility, even commanding me, "thou shalt not kill"' (Robbins, 1995, p. 66).

On the other hand, saying is also a direct and singular response to the other in which we personally attend to the other, a responsibility that no other can replace. Lingis (1994) uses two examples to describe the significance of saying as a direct and singular response to the other. One has to do with a situation in which we are speaking to someone who is dying. In this situation, there is an unbridgeable abyss between the one who lives and the one who is dying. The dying one becomes an absolute other with whom we share no experiences or of whose experiences we have no understanding, yet we are responsible to speak to him or her. We must choose to speak to the other. We stand alone, not as a member of a community with shared identities, but as the unique me that nobody can replace. What we say no longer matters; what matters is that we say something, as ourselves, with our own voices, to the dying. Lingis says, 'It does not matter what words we use—because there are, in a sense, no words. It only matters that we respond, that we take responsibility' (as cited in Biesta, 2004, p. 318). The other example has to do with a mother speaking to her infant. It shows how communication comes first as an expression. The mother 'cannot speak to the child with the borrowed, representative voice' (Biesta, p. 316) but has to speak as herself, and to the child alone. Her words or the sounds she makes are hers alone, with all the attentiveness and earnestness, while the meaning of the words or sounds is irrelevant. In these cases, saying and speaking as expression enables a personal, responsive relation to the other beyond words and meanings. To speak to the other means I am personally attending to the other, with my own voice, in this unfathomable human moment of profound difference. In speaking to the other, consequently, I become uniquely myself. Levinas locates the birth of human subjectivity in such encounters with the other. 'It is only in approaching the Other that I attend to myself. ... [As] responsible I am brought to my final reality' (p. 178). Or as Biesta says, 'It is ... this very way of speaking which constitutes me as a unique individual—as me, and no one else' (p. 317).

LEVINAS AND THE PHILOSOPHY OF EDUCATION

Listening

While Levinas has virtually neglected the listening aspect of discourse and its implication for human relations, in his early work, he did notice the power of sound and hearing on the self-mastering subject. 'In sound, and in the consciousness termed hearing, there is in fact a break with the self-complete world of vision ... To speak is to interrupt my existence as a subject and master' (Levinas, 1989, pp. 147, 149). Thus, in his attention to sound, he already hinted at the effect of listening, which is to disrupt the empire of the self and establish an intersubjective relation.

In recent years, there has been a growing interest among scholars in different fields, particularly educational philosophers, in the study of listening. What prompts this interest is that scholars have come to realize that, against the Western tradition that privileges a visual approach to the world, in the nature of listening, we may gain more insight into how to receive and respect others without imposition.

Traditionally, as Haroutunian-Gordon and Laverty (2011) note, the way of receiving the world in the West has been captured by 'visual metaphors' (p. 118). From Plato's cave to the metaphors of light and darkness, and to the 'enlightenment' movement, the Western 'viewing' and 'representing' approach to the world is apparent and has allowed the viewer to dominate and overpower the world and the other. In this approach, the other is often objectified, reduced, and their subjectivity compromised. As Levinas observes, 'Inasmuch as the access to beings concerns vision, it dominates those beings, exercises a power over them' (1969, p. 194). Extreme use of visual power can be seen in Foucault's description of gaze and surveillance.

In recent years, however, feminist scholars, critical race theorists, and theologians and counselors have all come to acknowledge the equal and ethical relation that may be cultivated in listening. Good listening does not dominate or intrude; rather, it allows a certain 'passivity' on the part of the listener and thus more respect for and less imposition on the speaker. In listening, as Waks (2010) suggests, we may be closer to our moral obligation to each other. While the focus of the study of listening is still mostly on logos, on connecting the heard to action, and on empathic understanding, are cognition of the noncognitive and expressive function of listening has also emerged. For example, in good listening, Waks (2010) observes, the listeners 'lay aside their roles and practical interests, ... suspend the category schemata ordinarily brought into play by them, ... [and forget] their preexisting identities' (p. 2748).

What I want to emphasize here is that, among our activities and interactions with others, listening appears to be the prime occasion for recognizing the originary, antecedent, and inexhaustible subjectivity of the speaker. It is in listening that we come to realize the impossibility of full and sure understanding; and it is in listening that the speaking other maintains his otherness, spontaneity, and originality—his subjectivity without truncation. Good listening is another mode of expressive use of language and discourse that provides opportunity for building Levinas's community of singularities.

Despite the West's traditional focus on logos and statements, the two aspects of the listening activity—the striving for understanding and the expressive receiving of the other in the other's unpredictable entirety—have, of course, been recognized even in classical investigations of dialog and listening. In a study of the dialog between

Socrates and Diotima in Plato's *Symposium*, Haroutunian-Gordon (2011) notes that, according to Plato, listening involves reasoning, 'drawing inferences about the implications of what one hears, ... trying to understand the meaning of what one hears' (p. 131), and identifying and resolving questions based on what one understands. However, in Socrates' listening to Diotima, he also found himself 'interrupted' at times, 'unable to draw an inference', and he had to form a new question that 'takes the listening in a different direction' (p. 131). In this case, even though Haroutunian-Gordon's emphasis is on the active role of the listener in responding to the speaker 'based upon the inference drawn about the meaning of what has been said—said now and previously' (p. 133), it is clear that the listener's interpretation and understanding is fragile and s/he has to be ready to modify, change, or even throw it away all together. S/he has to be ready to accept new directions and has to come up with new questions. In this listening process, the self cannot take the dominant role and does not single-handedly drive the conversation. Rather, the listener recognizes that s/he cannot predict what is to happen next, what is the entirety of the speaker's meaning, and the speaker, as the place of emission, remains unabsorbable and irreducible for the listener.

Thus in listening, as we listen to the speaking other, the speaker appears as a subject, immeasurable and inassimilable to our understanding. We inevitably become aware that the speaking other is more than what is said, more than what we can thematize and capture from the said, and we have no control over what is behind and beyond the said. The saying Other retains his/her subjectivity and otherness in our understanding. In good listening, more than in reading and seeing, the self is ready to be guided by the Other, receiving the Other as given, and the self's freedom and mastery is open to being interrupted. The encounter between a listener and a speaker, in the act of good listening, is 'a meeting of one whole being with another whole being', as Martin Buber suggests (Gordon, 2011, p. 208), and is the 'dialog [that] can only be grasped as an ontological phenomenon' (ibid.).

Beatty (1999) describes what happens in the activity of (good) listening. According to Beatty, not only does the good listener strive to 'grasp the precise meaning ... of the other without forcing, without reduction' (p. 284), the listener also recognizes that his/her understandings are 'tentative and fragile' constructions (p. 284). While attempting to comprehend the speaker's meanings, intentions, and experience in full, she recognizes the impossibility of such comprehension, and therefore to listen eventually becomes to respond 'to an *other*' (ibid., emphasis in the original). Good listening requires 'detachment' from the 'concerns, needs, interests' of the listener (p. 286) and the ability to suspend her judgment and 'claims to validity' (p. 287). The good listener has a '*moral-existential*' openness that allows herself, her character, to be transformed by the listening (p. 293). Above all, 'good listening is a way of permitting individuals to be themselves, even when their violation of our expectations or presumptions regarding them threatens our carefully erected ego-defenses and moral "holds" on the world' (p. 292). Thus, in good listening, the speaker's subjectivity is demonstrated and is recognized by the listener, and the freedom and totalizing power of the listener's ego and consciousness are interrupted.

Therefore, both in speaking and in listening, an ethical relation among unique human beings can be established, a relation not based on common substances and a relation enabling the signifying and receiving of human subjectivity and alterity without truncation. In this sense, the community of singularities can also be understood 'as a signifying encounter with difference' (p. 337), as Todd (2004) has proposed, because when we speak and listen attentively and respectfully to each other, we are forming a human community where all individuals maintain their irreducible subjectivity and alterity. Engaging in good listening and responsible speaking when we encounter different others is an ethical demand that we cannot escape and the ethical foundation of all other human activities. Such human community breaks out of totality and opens to all different others. The expressive use of language and discourse in the forms of speaking and good listening thus provides the possibility and practical guide to our social, political, and educational lives, particularly in a world of close encounters with radical differences.

Community, Democracy, and Education

Levinas's community, universality, and multiplicity are interchangeable ideas and his notion of community, where differences are appreciated and respected instead of a source of discrimination, paints an ideal picture of the democracy we have been striven for and have yet to realize. If a human community is a genuine multiplicity, democracy cannot be built upon a set of shared beliefs, values, abilities, or identity, but has to be built on our unconditional responsibility to each other as human beings. Levinas's idea that community is built upon our responsibility to the other—the responsibility to receive the other as who he/she is with all his/her otherness and uniqueness, and the responsibility to respond to his/her suffering and destitution— transforms the modern belief that democracy is based on isolated, self-mastering, and self-realizing subjects pursuing their own self interests. Democracy is no longer a battleground where we strategically further our own purposes but has to be an ethical space where communication and rational discussion on issues of common concern take place. What is particularly useful is Levinas's insight that language and discourse provide the means through which we can approach the other ethically and build a human society where all remain human subjects. The expressive use of language, prioritized by Levinas over rational language, enables a humane, ethical relation among singularities. By cultivating and reorienting the way we approach, speak, and listen to others, we can signify and receive each other as unique subjects with whom we engage in communication and rational debate. This view gives us a way to work with Habermas's communicative democracy but overcome his blind side where radical differences are difficult to account for (Zhao, 2014). If Habermas's communicative democracy can be realized at all, I argue, it has to be realized in the ethical space delineated by Levinas. In this sense, Levinas is quintessentially practical.

Contrasting sharply with this picture of democracy as ethical community is how democracy is often exercised in contemporary, democratic nations. While different parties and groups have the right and freedom to voice their ideas, little listening goes on in public debates. Parties are busy shouting their own ideas and distorting, purposefully or not, others' points and asserting that they have 'figured out' what the other party meant and wanted. Here, the purpose of speaking was to impose and enforce, and listening is virtually nonexistent. This is the democracy of self-projection and exclusion, and a practice of reducing and demeaning the other. To enact genuine democracy, then, we have a great deal to learn from Levinas.

Democracy that is situated in a Levinasian ethical space requires that we listen, earnestly and attentively, to the fullness and unpredictableness of others' expressions and experiences. It requires each of us to be open, even vulnerable, to acknowledge that our understanding of the others' points of view is incomplete and tentative, and to be ready to be redirected to new directions. But above all, we must listen in awe as if the words and expressions are coming from the inexhaustible and unknowable spring of their unique subjectivity. The others with whom we do not necessarily share the same point of view are nevertheless unique and irreducible human subjects calling for our highest respect. At the same time, we speak not to impose and enforce but to present ourselves as one human person attending to another. Speaking is first of all to offer ourselves in front of their humanness and dignity. Even if we do not speak the same language, we speak with a genuine voice of our own. With such expressive use of language from all parties, an ethical arena of irreducible and respected human beings is created, where comprehension and rational and critical debates may take place. Such an ethical area enables debates about justice and the common good. Democracy imagined in this way is radically transformed from its current form.

In education, Levinas's insights render the same transformation, particularly since in the contemporary age, schools are facing the great challenge of diversity. As Chinnery (2007) notes,

> While many North American classrooms prior to the1970s were, on the sur-
> face at least, quite homogeneous, shifting patterns of immigration, policies
> of racial integration, and mainstreaming of students with disabilities, as well
> as opening up discourse around race, class, gender, and sexuality, [have]
> brought differences to the fore. (p. 330)

It is no longer possible to follow Dewey's (1916) proposition in *Democracy and Education* that one of the chief aims of education is to enable young people to 'share in a common life' (p. 10). But educators are still relying on words and strategies such as 'inclusion', 'unity', 'sense of belonging', and 'connection' in building classroom communities. While recognizing differences, these strategies still value a sense of sameness and belonging and give students the perception that differences are undesirable and unwelcome because they do not belong. But when teachers can no longer expect to share or even to understand students' experiences, the search for understanding, empathy, and perspective-taking is deemed to fail because of the gap between 'us' and 'them'.

Levinas's ideas help us find a moral bond in the classroom when we might not share anything in common. Educational scholars have discussed at length that a school community should be conceived as a community of those who have nothing in common; that teachers should teach with ignorance, rather than with knowing and with empathy; and how to build a community where compassion is the essential moral disposition. My hope is that the discussion here can shed some light on the ways through which we can create a school and classroom community where students, newcomers with differences, are all received as unique human subjects, no matter how young or old they are, how much or how little knowledge they have, and how efficiently or inefficiently they speak our language. Instead of seeking a shared identity or common ground, or calling for understanding and empathy, therefore, we should first of all consider the classroom as an ethical space where students are welcomed, received, and appreciated for who they are—unique and irreducible human beings. The classroom is not a place for sameness, but the place of multiplicities, bound together by our unconditional responsibility to each other, to our singularity and subjectivity. Particularly in attentive listening and responsive speaking, we interact with each other, building the relationship of unique singularities. Without dismissing, ignoring, and judging, we open ourselves and listen to each other; and without violating, demeaning, and imposing, we address each other with genuine attentiveness, and speak with our own voices. We teach children to accept and appreciate difference through modeling the way we listen to them and present ourselves to them even though they are only children, and even if their otherness is beyond our expectations and presumptions.

After all, teachers and educators are responsible for making school a safe place for all newcomers. Responsive speaking and good listening are where we can start to build a classroom community where each student's unique and irreducible subjectivity and otherness is signified. Language is not just for transmitting meanings and knowledge. Prior to and above using language for knowing, assessing, and judging, language and discourse is first of all a human expression that enables ethical bonds among irreducible subjects. Through cultivating good listening, attentive speaking, and the sensitivity to recognize the irreducible subjectivity in the speaking others at school, we can make education a process through which students can eventually emerge as truly singular and irreducible human subjects. Levinas's ideas of community and expressive use of language, it seems, can really help us transform how we do education as well as democracy.

Disclosure statement

No potential conflict of interest was reported by the author.

References

Beatty, J. (1999). Good listening. *Educational Theory, 49*, 281–298.
Biesta, G. (2004). The community of those who have nothing in common: Education and the language of responsibility. *Interchange, 35*, 307–324.

LEVINAS AND THE PHILOSOPHY OF EDUCATION

Blanchot, M. (1993). *The infinite conversation*. (S. Hanson, Trans.). Minneapolis: University of Minnesota Press.

Caputo, J. (1997). *The prayers and tears of Jacques Derrida: Religion without religion*. Bloomington: Indiana University Press.

Chinnery, A. (2007). On compassion and community without identity: Implications for moral education. In D. Vokey (Ed.), *Philosophy of education 2006* (pp. 330–338). Urbana-Champaign, IL: Philosophy of Education Society.

Derrida, J. (1997). *Politics of friendship*. (G. Collins, Trans.). New York, NY: Verso.

Dewey, J. (1916). *Democracy and education*. New York, NY: The Free Press.

Elliott, B. (2009). Theories of community in Habermas, Nancy and Agamben: A critical evaluation. *Philosophy Compass, 4*, 893–903.

Gaon, S. (2005). Communities in question: Sociality and solidarity in Nancy and Blanchot. *Journal for Cultural Research, 9*, 387–403.

Gordon, M. (2011). Listening as embracing the other: Martin Buber's philosophy of dialogue. *Educational Theory, 61*, 207–219.

Haroutunian-Gordon, S. (2011). Plato's philosophy of listening. *Educational Theory, 61*, 125–139.

Haroutunian-Gordon, S., & Laverty, M. J. (2011). Listening: An exploration of philosophical traditions. *Educational Theory, 61*, 117–124.

Hegel, G. (2001). *Science of logic*. Retrieved from http://www.hegel.net/en/pdf/Hegel-Scilogic.pdf

Levinas, E. (1969). *Totality and infinity*. (A. Lingis, Trans.). Pittsburgh, PA: Duquesne University Press.

Levinas, E. (1989). The transcendence of words. In S. Hand (Ed.), *The Levinas Reader* (pp. 144–149). Cambridge, MA: Blackwell.

Lingis, A. (1994). *The community of those who have nothing in common*. Bloomington: Indiana University Press.

May, T. (1997). *Reconsidering difference: Nancy, Derrida, Levinas, and Deleuze*. University Park: The Pennsylvania State University Press.

Nancy, J. (1991). *The inoperative community*. (P. Gonnor, L. Garbus, M. Holland, & S. Sawhney, Trans.). Minneapolis: University of Minnesota Press.

Robbins, J. (1995). Aesthetic totality and ethical infinity: Lévinas on art. *L'Esprit Créateur, 35*, 66–79.

Todd, S. (2004). Teaching with ignorance: Questions of social justice, empathy, and responsible community. *Interchange, 35*, 337–352.

Waks, L. J. (2010). Two types of interpersonal listening. *Teachers College Record, 112*, 2743–2762.

Zhao, G. (2012). Levinas and the mission of education. *Educational Theory, 62*, 659–675.

Zhao, G. (2014). The public and its problem: Dewey, Habermas, and Levinas. *Journal of Educational Controversy, 8*(1). Retrieved from http://www.wce.wwu.edu/Resources/CEP/eJournal/v008n001/a006-PublicProblem.pdf

Zhao, G. (in press). From the philosophy of consciousness to the philosophy of difference: The subject for education after humanism. *Educational Philosophy and Theory*. doi: 10.1080/00131857.2015.1044840

Sound not Light: Levinas and the Elements of Thought

EMMA WILLIAMS & PAUL STANDISH

Abstract

Can Levinas' thought of the other be extended beyond the relation to the other human being? This article seeks to demonstrate that Levinas' philosophy can indeed be read in such a sense and that this serves to open up a new way of understanding human thinking. Key to understanding such an extension of Levinas' philosophy will be his account of the face and, more particularly, his claim that the relation to the face is 'heard in language'. Through explicating what is at stake in this claim, we will work to show how Levinas' philosophy leads us away from what might be called a tradition of understanding human thought through the medium of light (and hence intellection, theoria, contemplation) and takes us toward a conception of thinking that is conditioned by sound (and hence speech, language, and the sign). In the final section of the article, we consider what such a shift might suggest for the ways we understand thinking (and think of understanding) in both educational and everyday contexts.

> Absolute difference ... is established only by language. (Levinas, 1961/2004, p. 195)

> Thought is speech, and is therefore immediately face. (Derrida, 1968/2009, p. 125)

1. Introduction

At first glance, our topic may appear a strange one. What, one might wonder, does Levinas have to say about thinking? Alterity, subjectivity, ethics-before-ontology, certainly these are all familiar Levinasian concerns. But where and how does his philosophy have anything to say about human *thinking*? In response to these questions, we take further the possibility developed in earlier work that Levinas' thought of the other, configured through his account of the relation to the face, might be extended beyond the relation to the other human being (Llewelyn, 2000; Standish, 2009, p. 5). We do not want to deny that, for Levinas, the relation to the other is primarily and essentially cast as a relation to the other human being. Yet to what extent does Levinas' characterization of this relation to the other (human being) also necessitate a re-description of human *thinking*, insofar as thinking is already a relation to the other?

The aim of the present article is to demonstrate that Levinas' conception of the relation to the other can, indeed, be read in such a way. Key to understanding such an extension of Levinas' account will be what he says about language and, more specifically, about the role language plays within the encounter with the face (see Standish, 2009). Indeed, as we shall work to show in this article, through his casting of the relation with the face as one that is accomplished through language, Levinas works to re-describe the conditions of human relations in a way that simultaneously calls for a new understanding of human thought. We say a 'new' understanding of thought here so as to highlight the sense in which this conception will go beyond the way human thinking has been traditionally understood within the philosophical canon. Elsewhere, the authors of the present article have worked to explicate certain aspects of this traditional picture, and indicated how a number of philosophers work to get beyond it (see, e.g. Standish, 1992; Williams, 2013a, 2013b). Within this article, we are making a similar argument. Yet it can be said that, with the work of Emmanuel Levinas, this departure also comes to be cast in a particularly striking way. For Levinas' philosophy, as we shall see, works to move us beyond what can be called a tradition of understanding thinking (and of thinking of understanding) through the medium of *light*. Such a tradition is, to again anticipate what is to come, governed by an understanding of human thought in terms of intellection, *theoria*, assimilation, determination, and mastery. What Levinas moves us toward, by contrast, is a conception of thinking understood through the medium of *sound*. We are not yet in a position to understand this point fully, although it is clear that we are here invoking a shift in the elements—and a reconsideration of the relation between thought and language, idea and word.

It will be the task of sections four and five of this article to show how Levinas' philosophy accomplishes such a shift. In section six, we shall then turn to examine how such an understanding might inform our approaches to teaching and learning, and might problematize some of the more familiar approaches that are currently predominant in the sphere of 'thinking education' (understood, for example, in terms of thinking skills or critical thinking—see Williams, 2013a, 2013b). Before all of this, however, it will be worth our saying a little more about the traditional notion of thinking, which is afforded by the thematic of light. Indeed, it was through his own engagement with this familiar picture that Levinas himself came to move toward the otherness of the face, the sign, and the sound of thought.

2. Rays of Light

Let us begin, then, by sketching a traditional picture of human thought and experience. As we said above, this conception is one that takes its cue from the medium of light. What does this mean? Perhaps one way to begin answering this question is to

LEVINAS AND THE PHILOSOPHY OF EDUCATION

consider some of the ways in which the metaphor of light has prevailed within the philosophical canon, and more generally within Western thought. This task does not prove too difficult, for it is clear that a thematic of light finds early formulation in Plato's celebrated allegory of the cave, which depicts the ascent of a set of prisoners, from a dimly lit cave and world of shadows, up into the outside world, which is brightly lit by the sun. This story is, of course, used by Plato as a metaphor for man's ascent out of ignorance and illusion into the realm of knowledge and reality. And yet it is clear that, within this allegory, a connection is made between light, reality (as opposed to mere appearance or semblance), and the process of gaining knowledge of this reality. Indeed, the realm of appearance is depicted as one that takes place in the dim light of the cave fire, whereas the world of truth and reality is the illuminated world of the sun. Moreover, light itself is cast as a condition for moving out of the world of appearance—for it is by virtue of light that things are illuminated, shown as they really are, and hence made intelligible and sensible. As Plato himself puts it, knowledge is located in '... that region in which truth and real being brightly shine ...' (508d).

Within early modern philosophy, a similar conception of light is at play. Descartes conceived the *Meditations* as an attempt to reach a firm foundation for the sciences by means of a process of purely deductive *a priori* reasoning. And yet it soon becomes clear that at the origin of this self-secure, linear progression, is the moment of 'clear and distinct perception'—that which, as Descartes puts it, proceeds purely from his own intuition or the 'indubitable conception of a clear and attentive mind, which proceeds solely from the light of reason' (AT X 368). Clear and distinct perception is, of course, not synonymous with the perception yielded by the sense of vision or sight, which for Descartes was wont to be mistaken and deceived. This *inward-facing* perception proceeds not from the potentially fallible experience of the physical world but from the 'light of reason'—which is cast by Descartes as an indubitable and infallible source. Moreover, it is precisely such illuminated, infallible perceptions that give rise to Descartes' final acceptance of the existence of the material world. Hence, in his final meditation, Descartes reminds us that what we know of the material world remains *mediated* through our clear and distinct perceptions, that quasi-internal torch that shines forth and illuminates things as they really are, and not simply as they appear to be. Thus, whatever we clearly and distinctly perceive of the external world may be accepted as true; but what is not known in this way must be subjected to doubt and, in the final instance, cast out as mere illusion, fantasy, or error.

We could say much more. For one, we could invoke the philosophy of the Enlightenment, a term utilized to depict man's move out of immaturity and into self-sufficiency and autonomy. Here, as the name makes explicit, a thematic of light is connected to a process whereby one turns away from external authority and draws instead upon one's own intellectual capabilities to establish knowledge and determine what to believe. Yet in the interests of space, we should perhaps pass on here to another tradition in philosophy (and one that Levinas himself was greatly influenced by) namely, that of phenomenology.

The phenomenological project, as envisaged by its instigator Edmund Husserl, sought to offer a new description of human experience, one that would move away from metaphysical philosophizing and do justice to what is given in experience *as it is given*.[1] In this way, Husserl sought to return philosophical considerations to the realm of 'lived experience' and the 'things themselves'. A key feature of this move, in Husserl's philosophy, was the claim that human consciousness is always *intentional* (that is, is consciousness of something, that it has an object) and is thus constituted by and through a relation to what is *outside itself*. Such a characterization was hugely influential in its attempt to herald a new way of understanding human experience. As Jean-Paul Sartre declared, Husserl's insights restored to things 'their horror and their charm' and delivered us from the 'internal life' that appeared to govern philosophy as metaphysics (Sartre, 1939, p. 3). And yet, for all this, there remained questions over the extent to which Husserl's characterization of the acts of intentional consciousness was, in fact, adequately free from the assumptions of previous philosophy. In particular, and relevant to our concerns in this article, one might wonder whether Husserl's phenomenological description of consciousness in fact remained governed by a thematic of light. One area in which this largely appears to be the case is Husserl's characterization of intentional consciousness as that which *perceives the essences* of what it experiences. Indeed, this appears to cast our relation to the world as one that is ruled by *sight*, and hence appears to stress the representative and theoretical dimensions of human thought. Perhaps then, it could be said that phenomenology, as the term's root (*phos*, Gk.) suggests, remains in significant ways a philosophy of light—a description of human experience that is afforded by and made possible by virtue of the medium of light.

Perhaps one of the most well-known figures to have taken over Husserl's phenomenological project and sought to rectify the deficiencies with it was Martin Heidegger.[2] Heidegger's early philosophy endeavored to re-describe man's worldly comportment in terms of a 'being-in-the-world', a description that attempted to go beyond an overly theoretical and representative characterization of human experience and do justice to our everyday *engagement* in the world. Nevertheless, despite its advance over Husserl in a number of ways, there similarly have remained question marks over the extent to which Heidegger's thinking has a tacit commitment to certain thematics of previous metaphysical philosophy. In particular, once again, there is the suspicion that Heidegger's thinking contains a residual commitment to the light—as can perhaps be evidenced through his stress on notions such as disclosure and interpretation, and through later developments in his characterization of Being (as opposed to *beings*). Indeed Being, for Heidegger, is *Es gibt* (what gives ...): it has a bestowing and productive character; Being is the 'clearing' that brings things forth and allows them to shine forth.[3] Now, there are of course a number of complexities and subtleties within Heidegger's philosophy and, in particular, in his account of Being—that cannot be expanded upon within the present article. It is, however, perhaps enough for present purposes for us to note, along with John Llewelyn (1995), that certain features of Heidegger's philosophy might be read as still, 'in a strict sense', concerned with 'the giving and the given in light' (p. 24).

It is at this point that we can cross over to the philosophy of Emmanuel Levinas. For Levinas' thinking was itself greatly influenced by the phenomenological movement. And yet Levinas for crucial reasons also sought to move radically *away from* phenomenology—and from the politically problematic climate of Heideggerian philosophy in particular. In doing so, Levinas simultaneously worked to get beyond the philosophy of light. What reasons does Levinas have for seeking to move thus and what would such a move consist in? To answer these questions, let us further consider the picture of human experience that is afforded by the thematic of light.

3. Thought-Qua-Light

We would perhaps do well to utilize here a description of human experience that Levinas offers us in one of his early texts, *Existence and Existents*. Here, Levinas offers us a phenomenologically inspired picture of the relation between 'I and world' (Levinas, 1947/2003 pp. 27–44). As Levinas puts it, the Husserlian notion of intentionality, the conception of consciousness of ..., expresses this relation 'quite exactly' (p. 27). For our existence in the world is constituted by a relation to things, which we are attached to and which are wholly given to us (pp. 27–29).[4] These things, moreover and by virtue of this, function as the terminus of our intentions: they satisfy our intentions (p. 28). Hence, our relation to things in the world is, for Levinas, 'terribly sincere', we do not reach for things for the sake of something else, and we do not primarily maintain an abstracted or theoretical relation with things (p. 28). In eating this apple, for example, I am not acting for the sake of some higher purpose. Rather my act is a physical and visceral one, necessarily involving a number of sensations from the feelings of hunger gnawing away at my stomach to the taste of the apple as I bite. The possibility or fact of eating thus goes beyond a cognitive or theoretical relation—and such sincerity is typical, for Levinas, of existence in the world.

Notably, however, there is another feature of worldly existence for Levinas, which this last example brings out. This is, more specifically, the notion that worldly comportment is in many ways governed by *consumption*. Significantly, this consumption only runs *one way*—for in the intentional move toward things in the world, the I itself is not absorbed. Rather, as Levinas puts it, we maintain a distance from things in the world. Hence, while we seek to possess and consume things in the world, we are at the same time 'not overwhelmed by that possession' (p. 38). In our relation with the world, there is thus 'an attitude of reserve', an element of 'keeping one's hands free' (p. 39).

Significantly, Levinas suggests that what makes this kind of separation possible is the fact that our relation is here taking place through the medium of *light*. It is light that gives things to us, which makes them show up as destined 'for me' or usable 'by me'. Light thus makes possible the 'enveloping of the exterior by the inward'; it conditions and makes possible the acts of intentional consciousness (p. 41). And crucially, through this, Levinas brings us to see that this characterization of worldly comportment on one level connects up with traditional philosophical accounts of human experience. More specifically, as Levinas puts it, 'with the notions of the given, intentions and light, we rejoin the notion of knowing which Western thought uses to interpret consciousness' (p. 42).

Here, then, we come to add further formulation to what we stated above, viz. that the phenomenological attempt to go back to the things themselves in many ways retains a residual commitment to the thematics of illumination that have governed previous philosophy. Yet we are also able to say more here regarding what particular image of human thought and experience such a thematics affords. For as Levinas points out, by virtue of the light 'all the unfathomable mystery of a thing shows itself to us and is open to our grasp' (p. 33). Hence, human thought, qua light, becomes the activity of thematization and conceptualization. Through light, the world is made sensible and intelligible to the human 'subject'. And, through light, human beings thus come to do *violence* to the objects of thought—for, as Levinas puts it, the '"I think" comes down to "I can", to an appropriation of what is, to an exploitation of reality' (1961/2004, p. 46).

If, then, in the philosophical tradition 'the miracle of light is the essence of thought' (p. 41), we are here dealing with a thought that takes its cue and receives its character from the notions of determination, mastery, conceptualization, thematization, and representation. Such characterization appears, as we have seen above, to have been at work in philosophy even when it seeks to get beyond the prioritization of epistemology and the knowing relation, and return our considerations viscerally to the world of things. The question that concerns us in this article is whether it is possible to break free from this stranglehold. Can there be a conception of thinking that goes *beyond* the element of light? It is to this question that we shall now turn.

4. An Other Relation

As we stated at the outset, it is our contention in this article that Levinas' philosophy itself has the resource to move us beyond this conception of thought-qua-light. As we also stated, the key area that we need to attend to in order to see why this is the case is Levinas' account of the other. Now, this account is fairly well known in educational circles today. However, in this article, we shall be working to bring out a dimension of this account that is often overlooked. We shall come to see this more fully in the next section of this article. For now, however, let us move toward this by tracing some of the more familiar aspects of Levinas' account of the other.

Levinas characterizes the relation with the other as a relation with the *face*—an encounter in which I am confronted with that which radically exceeds myself. Notably, in casting the relation in this way, Levinas proposes an account of intersubjectivity that differs quite significantly from that of previous philosophies and phenomenologically inspired philosophies in particular. For Husserl, in encountering the other, I experience a being who is perceived to be *like me,* hence the other appears on the plane of my intentional consciousness as an *alter ego*. Heidegger, on the other hand, characterized our relation with other people in terms of *mitsein* (being-with), thus, suggesting a relation of the side-by-side, of community and collectivity, or perhaps of solidarity, to include the currently more fashionable term. Levinas' account of the face, in contrast to both of these, stresses the radical *alterity* of the other. For the face, Levinas claims signals an interiority that I can never reach or subsume; it directs me toward the impassable distance between me and the other person that not even the closest spatial proximity could transverse.

Levinas is struck by Vasily Grossman's description in *Life and Fate* of the way people who were standing in line before the notorious gate in Lubyanka, from which one could get news of loved ones arrested for political crimes, could read 'on the nape' of the person in front of them 'the feelings and hopes of his misery' (Morgan, 2011, p. 19). The back of the neck is exposed, unprotected, undefended: this too is part of what Levinas evokes in the idea of the face, such that the literal face serves as a kind of metonym for this larger human vulnerability. The face, like the nape, expresses to us the frailty, weakness, and mortality of the other. To see the face is already to have seen this vulnerability and interiority. It is in this way that, as Levinas claims, the face already confronts us as an *ethical command*: it summons me to responsibility before the other and to an obligation that deepens the more I answer to it. This is not, importantly, to be understood as an incidental relation—say, where we come across the other in an unfortunate situation. People always are vulnerable, not just possibly but inevitably so. Such is the human condition. For Levinas, then, the relation with the face is the primordial structure of our relation with other people: it is what conditions and makes possible all our further relations.

While the encounter with the face is an experience of something that is before us, while it is an experience with something physically confronting us, we should understand the nature of this confrontation carefully. It is, Levinas says, a 'concrete abstraction'. Now, the term 'concrete' here points us to the way in which the account of the face is intended to do justice to our *actual experience* of the other—it should not be understood as a (philosophical) abstraction that turns us away from the real individual, from the physical encounter with the face, and toward a generalized other. However, and as the phrase also suggests, there is a sense in which the relation with the face is at the same time an *abstraction*. For Levinas is not here depicting an encounter in which one becomes fixated upon a particular person who, in virtue of their particular characteristics, is the object of our concern, and where, say, one gazes into the depths of the other's eyes in a heightened moment of awareness and empathy. To encounter the face is not to fix our gaze upon the particular features of another's face such as the color of their eyes or the shape of their face: to see the face is not to see the color of the eyes. In fact, the face itself radically *exceeds* and *overflows* its physical determination. The face is there in the nape of the neck and, as we shall see, in the approach of language.

But with this last point, we are introduced to a thought that is admittedly complex. For in what way and in what sense can we understand this excessive and overflowing quality of the face? The question is a significant one. Indeed, we would argue that it is, in fact, through this point that we are brought to see how Levinas' account of the face has import beyond what can be said only about our *relations* with other people—for it also refers us to something significant about the nature of human thought itself. (As if we could without thought even exist as people. And in any case without thought what could the world possibly be?) Let us now turn to explore this more fully.

5. The Sound of the Face

As we have shown in section two, human thought itself as intentional is always already a relation to the other (and this of course includes the other human being), even where that thought is abstract and theoretical. The thematic of light, as we have seen, affords a certain characterization of this relation—one that takes its cue from representation, comprehension, assimilation, and thematization. The question that now concerns us is: Does Levinas' philosophy open to an alternative view?

We have already started to move some way toward seeing that it does through our consideration of what Levinas says about the relation to the face. Yet clearly there is reason to say more. What constitutes the relation to the face? In particular, we can say something about the way Levinas characterizes the *conditions* that make the relation with the face possible, and about the force of the confrontation the image implies, through which I find myself already addressed, called to response. It is here that we move toward a shift in the elements. For it can be said that what conditions Levinas' account of alterity is, to be sure, not light but *sound*. And this characterization is there recurrently in Levinas' words: the relation to the face is not realized in abstract contemplation but is 'heard in language' (1961/2004, p. 297). And I am always already addressed.

We will need to do some work in order to understand precisely what Levinas is referring us to here. Let us note initially that, through this characterization, Levinas suggests that language cuts across the realm of light—that sphere constituted by the categories of the contemplative subject and the external object—and hence moves us beyond representation, appropriation, thematization, and conceptualization. Now, initially, this might sound like a strange point to make about language. Indeed, on the strength of a traditional reading, wherein language is taken to be a communicative instrument and is hence given the 'servile function of translating ... pre-existing thought', it would appear that language precisely plays such a representative role. Of course, with his claim that the relation to the other is 'heard in language', Levinas is not seeking to deny that such a function is there. Yet he is seeking to bring out a further, and perhaps more essential, dimension of language. This is the way language functions as *expression* and *invocation*. This dimension is perhaps most clearly evidenced, as Levinas himself suggests, in the act of being spoken to or being addressed. When I am addressed, language does not, to be sure, function merely as representation or communication by way of some lifeless sign. Rather a condition of being addressed is that I am approached by what is exterior to myself, otherwise than myself. We shall come to say a little more on this point in a moment. For now, let us note that, in this way, Levinas comes to draw a connection between language (understood in its invocative sense) and the face. More exactly, for Levinas, the relation with the face is *inseparable* from speech; to be confronted by the face is to be confronted by someone who speaks, who addresses me. Indeed, would it be possible to see someone's face without at the same time knowing that this is someone who speaks? We might of course be able to do this via a thought experiment or some other abstraction from the primary situation. But for such abstraction to be possible there must have first been the recognition of the other as one who speaks. Indeed, the very possibility of communicating and conversing with others, upon which our everyday life is built, is itself predicated upon this initial casting of the other as one who speaks—for what would be the point of speaking to someone if we did not think they were themselves capable of speech? More radically, what could our speaking be? What could we be?

LEVINAS AND THE PHILOSOPHY OF EDUCATION

In fact in 1976, in a lecture series at the Sorbonne (Levinas, 2000), in the wake of the publication of *Otherwise than Being* (Levinas, 1974/1978), Levinas reprises the theme of sincerity, introduced, as we saw, in *Existence and Existents*, but here in a way that moves beyond the satisfactions identified there. Sincerity is now found not in the eating of the apple, the satisfactions of consumption or possession, but in a breaking open of this sensuous-affective relation, even to the giving of bread taken from one's mouth. Language is not then to be understood in terms of any putative fit with a pre-existing 'objective' reality, to which it is adequate and wherein it finds satisfaction; rather, in its essential temporalization, it creates meaning and world. *Saying* then is always a movement away from any ossification of the *said*. 'To make signs to the extreme point of making a sign of oneself' is to resist the dispersal of the *logos* in possibilities of being (Levinas, 2000, p. 192). Such saying is not explainable in terms of partnership in dialog or exchange of information. It is rather to be understood in terms of 'a passivity of passivity' (p. 191), of the accusative 'I', realized in the French expression *Me voici* (literally, 'See me here'; otherwise, 'Here I am'). The ethic imperative in the passivity of this reception of the other is always there, logical precondition to any dialogue or communication. It imparts a truthfulness prior to the making of true statements. Its sincerity is not an *act* of exposing but a matter of 'exposing the exposure' (*ibid.*), a giving that exhausts our reserves.

> The subject is sensitive to the pro-vocation that was never presented but that struck it with a trauma ... Therein lies a heteronomy, in this relationship with another where I am, myself, torn from my beginning in me, from my equality with myself. This heteronomy is an alteration that is not alienation, not slavery, not a loss of uniqueness, since precisely no one may replace me, since I am chosen. (p. 193)

This breaking open realized in the saying, however much we may deny or attempt to override it, is the condition of subjectivity and hence constitutive of the relation to the other.

Certainly these are dizzying thoughts, but they should leave us with no doubt of the place that Levinas accords to language as speech. Specifically, the experience of the face is *itself* the experience of speech, of invocation, of being called, of saying. Hence, whatever different materializations language can subsequently assume, its primordial element is sound. And with this, crucially, we also come to understand more fully what is at stake in the *alterity* of the other that we glimpsed in the previous section. Let us steady the tone a little by thinking more simply about the nature of signs.

Consider first the way in which speech, and more generally language itself insofar as language is a system of signs, always involves a reference to something beyond itself. More specifically, as structuralist and post-structuralist philosophers have pointed out, the sign is what it is by virtue of its difference from *other* signs; hence, we never grasp signs as they are 'in themselves'. Of course, signs do have a material form; they are constituted by a particular sound sequence, for example, or via certain marks on a page. Yet signs are not themselves *reducible* to their particular material form—as can be shown from the way that one can say 'day' in a loud or a soft voice, at a high or low pitch, and the word will still, within certain limits, be recognizable.

Indeed, what makes it possible for the sound sequence that is produced when one says 'day' to function as a signifier is the fact that it can be distinguished from the sound sequence that is made when one says 'way' or 'lay' or 'bay' for example. A similar point can be made with regard to the written sign. Indeed, one can recognize the letter 'b' even if it is written in a number of different ways, using different fonts, and different sizes:

$$b\ b\ \mathbf{b}\ \mathbf{b}\ b\ \boldsymbol{b}\ \boldsymbol{b}$$

What makes these particular marks recognizable as instances of the letter 'b' is, indeed, that they are *not* instances of the letter 'a' or 'c'. Yet from this it becomes clear that signs, spoken words included, necessarily remain unsaturated and unconsummated. As Jacques Derrida puts it, signs are, by nature, always 'delayed' or 'deferred': the very nature of the sign 'is not to be proximate to itself'. Signs are thus, we might say, constituted via an absence.

Now, all of this refers us to something important about the relation with the face. For in and through language, and speech is no exception, we are called by something which remains *beyond* our comprehension and grasp. Levinas himself attests to such a relation, stating that 'absolute difference … is established only by language' (1961/2004, p. 195). Yet if the relation with the face is itself one that is inseparable from speech, and is accomplished in speech, then it must be the case that this *is itself a relation with absolute difference*—with what is not fully given and goes beyond my comprehension and grasp. And it is in this way that we come to understand what is at stake in Levinas' claim that the relation with the face is a relation with what refuses 'to be contained', with what is 'forever outside', and could never 'be converted into interiority' (p. 295). For the face, like the sign and by virtue of its being inseparable from the sign, has an interiority that I cannot and will never fathom or assimilate. Hence, while it is the case that I can *see* another face, that the face is given to sight and vision, the face also *exceeds* its particular material form; it is not proximate to or given through its material form.[5] As Levinas puts it, the face 'breaks through the form that nevertheless delimits it' (p. 198). It is hence an 'overflowing, irreducible to an image of overflowing'—phrasing that might fruitfully be compared to Derrida's evocation of the 'non-saturation' and 'dissemination' of the sign: its bursting open with possibilities of meaning and interpretation.

In this way, we come to understand why the relation with the face must be one that takes place not in the light, but in *sound*. For we would not do justice to the relation with the face if we considered this under the glare of light—that which gives everything over to us but in such a way that it yields to or feeds our tendencies toward assimilation and domination. The relation with the face is an experience of the appresented, the unpresentable; hence, it must be realized in language. And as such, as Levinas points out, the relation with the face should not, strictly speaking, be called an *experience* at all. For the term 'experience' presupposes an encounter with something that is fully given to us, and is present to us; it presupposes that which can be comprehended, grasped, and known. Yet the face is precisely not like this. The face escapes and eludes our 'sensory experience'—at least in the way sense experience is typically theorized about, especially in terms of atomistic experiences of seeing, hearing, touching, and so on. It is not illuminated, or 'given to vision'. The relation with the face is, rather, accomplished in the structural non-presence of expression, the sign, and language.

Can we say any more? More specifically, can we draw out the implications of this account of the face further? Indeed we can. And this is because, as we have noted in the previous section, the relation with the face should not be understood as merely *one* aspect of human experience amongst others. The relation with the face is not a merely *incidental* and *occasional* relation. Rather, Levinas takes it to be *the very condition of human experience in the first place*. Hence, we can say that the relation with the face conditions *human thinking itself* (in that this is already a relation to the other). Indeed, Levinas himself emphasizes the fundamental 'solidarity' between thought and speech—drawing as he does upon Maurice Merleau-Ponty's conception that 'disincarnate thought, thinking speech before speaking it, thought constituting the world of speech ... was a myth' (1961/2004, pp. 205–206). And in this way, we come to see how Levinas' account of the relation with the other can be read as offering a new conception of human thought. This is a conception that radically departs from the traditional picture of thought-qua-light. For indeed, as we might put it utilizing Derrida's phrasing, Levinas' philosophy opens us to the view that 'thought is language' and 'is thought in an element analogous to sound not to light' (Derrida, 1968/2009, pp. 125).[6] Here, then, we are moved toward a re-description of what happens when we think. For if thought operates qua sound, then our thinking will be less under our control than it was within the realm of light. To acknowledge this is to build on the phenomenological insight—there, for example, in Heidegger's *Being and Time* (Heidegger, 1962)—that, whereas to a large extent, we control what we see by the movements of our head (including those of our eyelids and our eyes themselves), our hearing is not so autonomously regulated: sounds come to us from behind and surprise us, and we do not, for the most part, move our ears. To look is to concentrate the attention by directing the gaze and focusing the eyes; to listen is also to attend, but in a manner more passive and receptive, open to what one happens to hear. What I see is the object of my gaze, while the sounds I hear envelop me. As Levinas himself puts it, and like the sound that catches me unawares, 'signification surprises the very thought that thought it' (1961/2004, p. 206). But the phenomenological contrast exposes a more metaphysical difference: specifically, that thinking (qua sound) will no longer be understood as secured by that stable, permanent, Archimedean point from which we can view the world, but will rather be recognized as open, dynamic, and fluid. Thought-qua-sound will be something that does not depend upon what is permanently given, what is present, and what endures, but on what fades and passes into nothingness, just as speech depends on the fading of syllable after syllable. And yes, again following phenomenological insights, as indicated in Heidegger's title *Being and Time*, this is to emphasize the temporal, not the spatial: it constitutes a freeing from the ocular obsessions that came to the fore with the rise of science, just as it is a renunciation of the more or less Platonist expectations of full presence, spatial and temporal, that have dominated Western thought. By understanding thinking through the element of sound, we will no longer connect thought with the traditional notions of *psyche*, *theoria*, or intellect. Indeed, thought-qua-sound invokes more readily a thematic of breath, of inspiration, of *pneuma*, which brings us, following the Latin (Christian) tradition, into the realm of the spirit—which, like the sign, is what it is by virtue of what it is *not*, by virtue of *absence*. There is much more that could be said on this. Perhaps, however, we are already saying more than we are permitted to in the present context. Let us then, by way of drawing this article to a close, turn to consider how this new conception of thought might play out in our everyday human practices, and in our educational practices in particular.

6. Elements of Thought

In education today, there is a predominant tendency to talk about, and indeed try to bring about, the improvement of thinking in terms of notions such as 'critical thinking', 'thinking skills', and in some quarters 'philosophy for children'. What is foregrounded in such fields is, as we have suggested elsewhere (Williams, 2013a, 2013b), *a particular and limited way of thinking*: such thinking relies on the generic procedures of logic and epistemology, and is almost exclusively concerned with the quasi-technical activities of constructing arguments, formulating demonstrations, assessing and evaluating claims by way of set criteria, and so forth. What we think *about*, on such a view, is, simultaneously, made to appear as data, quantifiable propositions, or statements that are subject to our scrutiny and control. Hence, we stand well back from the things we are thinking about and learn to approach and relate to the world in a manner that is claimed to be objective, reflective, and critical.

Such tendencies operate upon an understanding of thinking that takes its cue from the element of *light*. For here, we are in the realm of a subject who stands apart from the things she is thinking about; who consumes them without being consumed by them; and who thus thinks while 'keeping her hands free'. Moreover, we are in the realm of thinking as assimilation, conceptualization, and thematization—activities at which we human beings are, of course, undeniably good and toward which we are, like the moth to the flame, undeniably drawn.

Such an understanding of thinking—and of what is thought *about*—is increasingly prevalent not only within the field of thinking education. The call to stand back and gain a critical, reflective perspective on things (and, indeed, on ourselves insofar as we are one of the 'things' we can think about) is one that is made upon us in many areas of life today. Hence, the human resources manager shortlists applicants for a role by means of a quantified rating system; the new employee undergoes an appraisal that measures her successes (and failures) against predefined criteria; the uncertain fiancée draws up a list of the pros and cons of her potential partner to aid her in making her big decision. In each of these cases, the possibilities are limited by structures that, in many ways, work as a convenient substitute for thought itself.

We have sought to open an account of thinking that goes beyond this picture. Via Levinas' notion of the other, we have come to a conception of thinking that is conditioned not by light, but by *sound*. This means, as we saw at the close of the previous section, that human thinking is made possible by means of a relation to that which is appresented, held back, and beyond ourselves. And of course, through this, we also come to re-describe what it is that we are thinking *about*—for, *qua* sound, things cannot be understood simply as objects fully given to us, to be brought entirely under our control and domination. Thus, we come to recognize that the job applicant is indeed more than the criteria she is defined by; the new employee is indeed more than the successes and failures defined by the appraisal form; and the potential husband is indeed more than the sum of pros and cons drawn up on the hesitant fiancée's list. It might be objected that this much is *obvious*—for surely we have known all the time that a person is more than a quantified number or a list of pros and cons? Yet by virtue of the increasing stress on reductive modes of thinking, such obviousness can, paradoxically, come to be overlooked. Moreover, it can be said that the *teaching* of thinking, predominantly in terms of the discourse of critical thinking or 'thinking skills', heightens the possibility of such forgetfulness by shoring up the idea that it is only thinking of this kind that provides a rigorous and robust way of proceeding.

As our analysis of Levinas has shown, then, to construe human thought in this way is to fail to do justice to the otherness that conditions and makes such abstracted relations possible in the first place. Put simply, it is to fail to do justice to the *elements* of thought. It is to be deaf to the fact that, before light, there is sound.

Disclosure statement

No potential conflict of interest was reported by the authors.

Notes

1. Of course, much could be said about the idea of the given. Wilfred Sellars famously introduced the phrase 'the myth of the given', yet in phenomenological philosophy, and in Heidegger in particular, as we shall come to see, the given, characterized through the *Es gibt* (*it gives* ...), takes on a more animated sense.
2. As is well known, Levinas' relation with Heidegger was itself complex.
3. Heidegger draws attention approvingly to Aristotle's explication of discourse in terms of *apophainesthai*, letting something be seen, while his later elaboration of the notion of the clearing alludes obliquely, though more obviously than is evident in English, to the *Aufklärung, the Enlightenment*.
4. It is worth pointing out here that Levinas is referring to 'things' as opposed to 'objects'. In this way, Levinas is following Heidegger's conception that our relation to the world is not primarily a theoretical or epistemological relation, but is rather a relation with *things* that are 'ready-to-hand'. For more on this see Williams (2013a) and Standish (1992, 1997).
5. In fact, we can say too that our ordinary seeing is itself something beyond the abstracted physical sense that we construct in our theorizations. We return to this point below.
6. Of course, the sense of analogy that the quotation from Derrida invokes here is not analogy as it is normally understood. The relation for Levinas between thought and sound is not merely analogical, for the two are inseparable.

References

Derrida, J. (1968/2009). Violence and metaphysics. In J. Derrida (Eds.), *Writing and difference* (pp. 78–97). London: Continuum.

Heidegger, M. (1962). *Being and time*. (J. Macquarrie, & E. Robinson, Trans.). Oxford: Basil Blackwell.

Levinas, E. (1947/2003). *Existence and existents*. Pittsburgh: Duquesne University Press.

Levinas, E. (1961/2004). *Totality and infinity*. Pittsburgh: Duquesne University Press.

Levinas, E. (1974/1978). *Otherwise than being or beyond essence*. (A. Lingis, Trans.). Boston, MA: Kluwer Academic.

Levinas, E. (2000). *God, death, and time*. (B. Bergo, Trans.). Stanford, CA: Stanford University Press.

Llewelyn, J. (1995). *Emmanuel Levinas: The genealogy of ethic*. London: Routledge.

Llewelyn, J. (2000). *The Hypocritical Imagination: Between Kant and Levinas*. London: Routledge.

Morgan, M. L. (2011). *The Cambridge introduction to Emmanuel Levinas*. Cambridge: Cambridge University Press.

Sartre, J. P. (1939). Intentionality: A fundamental idea of Husserl's phenomenology. Retrieved from http://www.mccoyspace.com/nyu/12_s/anarchy/texts/03-Jean-Paul_Sartre-Intentionality.pdf

Standish, P. (1992, January). *Beyond the self: Wittgenstein, Heidegger, and the limits of language*. Aldershot: Ashgate, viii + 275.

Standish, P. (1997). Heidegger and the technology of further education. *Journal of Philosophy of Education, 31*, 439–460.

Standish, P. (2009). *Lévinas and the language of the curriculum, Lévinas and Education: At the intersection of faith and reason*. London: Taylor and Francis.

Williams, E. (2013a). 'Ahead of all beaten tracks': Ryle, Heidegger and the ways of thinking. *Journal of Philosophy of Education*, 53–70.

Williams, E. (2013b). Out of the ordinary: Incorporating limits with Austin and Derrida. *Educational Philosophy and Theory*. Published online ahead of print Retrieved from http://www.tandfonline.com/doi/full/10.1080/00131857.2013.828580

The Rediscovery of Teaching: On robot vacuum cleaners, non-egological education and the limits of the hermeneutical world view

GERT BIESTA

Abstract

In this article, I seek to reclaim a place for teaching in face of the contemporary critique of so-called traditional teaching. While I agree with this critique to the extent to which it is levelled at an authoritarian conception of teaching as control, a conception in which the student can only exist as an object of the interventions of the teacher and never as a subject in its own right, I argue that the popular alternative to traditional teaching, that is to make the teacher a facilitator of learning, is insufficient. The reason for this has to do with the fact that learning, understood as a process of interpretation and comprehension, ultimately also does not allow the student to exist as a subject. I provide support for this point through a reading of two articles by Emmanuel Levinas in which he puts forward the case that our subjectness is not generated through our own acts of signification, but is rather constituted from the outside, that is, through the address of the other. It is in this event, where a different conception of teaching emerges—one that, unlike authoritarian teaching and unlike self-generated adaptive learning, is precisely aimed at making the subjectness of the student possible.

Un élève-sujet est capable de vivre dans le monde sans occuper le centre du monde. [A student-subject is able to live in the world without occupying the centre of the world.] (Meirieu, 2007, p. 96)

What is Actually Wrong with Traditional Teaching?

This is an article about teaching and learning. But unlike so many articles that have been published over the past fifteen to twenty years, it is not an article in which I will

This is an Open Access article distributed under the terms of the Creative Commons Attribution License (http://creativecommons.org/licenses/by/4.0/), which permits unrestricted use, distribution, and reproduction in any medium, provided the original work is properly cited.

follow the all too familiar line of argument in which so-called 'traditional' teaching—that is, a staging where the teacher speaks and students are supposed to listen and passively absorb information—is seen as bad and outdated, and where something allegedly more modern, focused on the facilitation of students' learning—either individually or in some kind of dialogical process—is seen as good, desirable and 'of the future'. While the opposition between 'traditional' and 'contemporary' is itself already a bit stale, we should not forget how traditional the critique of traditional teaching actually is. John Dewey already made the point, as did Jan Ligthart in the Netherlands and many educators and educationalists before and after them. The critique is also not entirely valid, because even in classrooms where teachers speak and students sit quietly, a lot of things are actually happening on the side of the students—they may of course feel bored, alienated or ignored, but they may also feel challenged, fascinated and inspired; who knows? I also wonder whether anyone has actually ever suggested that education *operates* as a process of transmission and passive absorption, even if it is *staged* in this way. Here, I agree with Virginia Richardson, that 'students also make meaning from activities encountered in a transmission model of teaching' (Richardson, 2003, p. 1628).

In light of the critique of traditional teaching, it is, of course, also ironic that some of the currently most popular technology-mediated forms of education—such as TED talks, MOOCs and the numerous amateur instructional videos on YouTube—are all staged in 'conventional' ways, that is, with someone talking and explaining so that others can watch, listen and learn. One could even ask whether the endless stream of worksheets and individual and group tasks that have invaded the contemporary classroom—from preschool to higher education—is not beginning to trivialise education, just turning it into busy work. And we should not forget those momentous examples of traditional, one-way forms of communication—from Socrates's apology, via Lincoln's Gettysburg address, to the speeches of Barack Obama—where, to my knowledge, no one has actually ever complained about the absence of study questions or group work that would allow the audience to make personal sense of what has been said. In this regard, I believe that we really should not underestimate our capacity to receive.

What these observations begin to suggest is that there actually may be something wrong with the ongoing critique of traditional teaching. But making this point, and trying to establish a more general case for the re(dis)covery of teaching (see Biesta, 2012a), is fraught with difficulties. This is not least so because nowadays the most vocal arguments for teaching and the teacher come from the conservative end of the political spectrum, where they are aimed at re-establishing the kind of order and control that apparently is lacking in modern society and modern education (for a different take on this issue, see Meirieu, 2007). This seems to suggest that the only *progressive* alternative lies in the demise of the teacher—and more precisely the demise of 'traditional' teaching—and a turn towards learning; a turn where the teacher only exists as a facilitator of otherwise 'autonomous' learning processes. (I use 'autonomous' here to refer to the idea that these processes are supposed to be going on anyway, irrespective of the presence of the teacher.)

LEVINAS AND THE PHILOSOPHY OF EDUCATION

The problem here, if I see it correctly, has to do with the binary construction of options, that is, with the idea that the only meaningful response to authoritarian forms of teaching lies in the abolition of teaching and a turn towards learning. It is just remarkable that the third option, namely that of reconstructing our understanding of teaching and the teacher along progressive lines, is hardly ever considered. Yet it in is this third option—an option which relies on the idea that freedom is not the opposite of authority or an escape from authority, but has to do with establishing a 'grown up' relationship with what may have authority in our lives; a process in which authority becomes *authorised*, as Meirieu (2007, p. 84) has put it—that we can see the beginnings of an entirely different response to authoritarian forms of teaching, be they traditional, be they progressive.

In this article, I engage with one dimension of the urgent and complex task of the re(dis)covery of teaching. I do this by means of an exploration of what we might term the anthropological[1] dimensions of the discussion, that is, of underlying assumptions about the human being and its place in the world. I embark on this with some trepidation, because I neither think that anthropology is a matter of choice—it is not that we can simply choose how we want to understand the human being and then can happily proceed from there—nor that anthropology is a matter of grounding—where, once we know what the human being really is, we can put education on a safe and secure path. My ambition with this article is to make visible what the prevailing conception of the human being is—first and foremost in our educational imaginary, but the impact is a wider one—and to suggest that such a conception is neither necessary nor inevitable by indicating how the human being and its place in the world might be approached differently. (I deliberately use the word 'approached' here because, as I will argue in what follows, this is not a matter of *understanding* the human being differently; the challenge rather is an existential one.) Through this I not only seek to create the possibility for developing a different understanding of teaching, but I also seek to show how teaching—or, to be more precise: the experience of being taught (Biesta, 2013a)—reveals something important about our human existence. This will allow me to suggest that in the demise of teaching and the teacher, there is actually more at stake than only an educational problematic and a problematic that would only concern the school.

The underlying structure of my argument is fairly simple, but I admit that the detail is more complex. I start from the contention that to the extent to which the critique of traditional teaching is a critique of teaching as control, this critique is educationally valid as it shows that in traditional teaching, the student can only appear as object of the teacher's interventions, but never as a subject in its own right (which is also what Freire objects to in banking education, see Biesta & Stengel, in press). I then argue that the suggestion that we can overcome this problem by focusing on students and their learning—understood as acts of interpretation and comprehension—fails, because such acts of interpretation and comprehension have an egological structure that emanates from the self and returns to the self, even if this occurs 'via' the world. For this reason, I suggest that in acts of interpretation and comprehension, the self can still not appear as subject, but remains an object in relation to its environment. I suggest, in more philosophical terms, that our subjectness is not constituted through acts of signification. This insight I take from the work of Levinas, who provides the main source of inspiration for this article. With Levinas, I suggest that our subjectness is rather called for from the 'outside'—which is why I discuss the theme of 'transcendence'—and has to do with the 'event' of 'being addressed'. It is this event where a different meaning of teaching manifests itself, one where the student can appear as subject rather than object. And it is this sense of teaching that I seek to (re)discover in this article.

Overcoming the Egological World view

I proceed in this article by means of a reading of two texts from Emmanuel Levinas, the philosopher who, in my view, has contributed most to exposing the limitations of the 'egological' world view, that is, the way of thinking that starts from the (assumption of the existence of the) self as self-sufficient ego or consciousness, in order *then* to thematise everything that is 'outside the subject' (Levinas, 1994). However, Levinas's thought is not a simple reversal of this gesture, but comes closer to what elsewhere I have referred to as an 'ethics of subjectivity' (Biesta, 2008). The idea of an ethics of subjectivity hints at a double shift. First of all, it indicates that Levinas seeks to approach the question of human subjectivity through ethics rather than through knowledge. There is, in other words, no *theory* about the subject, no cognitive claim about what the subject *is*. Yet this also means that Levinas's writings should not be read as a 'traditional' ethical philosophy or theory of ethics as what is at stake is the question of human subjectivity or subjectness.[2] In this sense, we can say that his writings neither prescribe nor describe what being ethical or acting ethically is.

Rather modestly—particularly compared to the rich flow of language through which Levinas tries to 'capture' something of the mystery of human subjectness—Levinas somewhere says that he 'describe[s] subjectivity in ethical terms' (Levinas, 1985, p. 95). Key in this effort is his suggestion that responsibility is 'the essential, primary and fundamental structure of subjectivity' (Levinas, 1985, p. 95). He emphasises, however, that responsibility here 'does not supplement a preceding existential base' (Levinas, 1985, p. 95). It is not that the subject first exists—as a self-sufficient, egological subject—and then encounters a responsibility or takes a responsibility upon itself. It is rather, as Levinas puts it, that 'the very node of the subjective is knotted in ethics understood as responsibility' (Levinas, 1985, p. 95). Responsibility, in the words of Bauman (1993, p. 13), thus appears as 'the first reality of the self'. It is the moment where the self finds itself, so to speak. Or to be even more precise, it is the moment where the self *matters* because in its responsibility the self is 'non-interchangeable' (Levinas, 1985, p. 101).[3]

That Levinas's ethics of subjectivity is not to be understood as a theory about the human subject already indicates some of the difficulties with trying to overcome egological ways of thinking and being. After all, if we simply were to issue a different theory or different truth about the subject—for example by arguing that the self has a social origin—we would decentre the self at the level of our theory, but would still be doing this from a centre, that is, the centre from which we issue such a theory. We would therefore performatively deny—'that there is a centre from which I can issue the truth'—the very thing we would declaratively deny—'that no such centre exists'. Before I discuss how Levinas engages with this difficulty, I wish to say a few things about what I see as the prevailing educational imaginary, particularly in order to show its fundamentally egological character.

On Robot Vacuum Cleaners, Learning Environments and the Hermeneutical World view

One way in which we might characterise the prevailing educational imaginary is in terms of robot vacuum cleaners. This idea came to me after a conversation with a scholar working in the learning sciences who raised questions about my critique of the language of learning in education (for example in Biesta, 2010); a critique which, to a certain extent, he read as a critique of the very idea of learning itself (which I think is correct; see Biesta, 2013b). What, so he asked, could be wrong with or educationally unhelpful about the study of intelligent adaptive systems? While I was happy to concede that nothing is wrong with the study of such systems as such, my question was whether such systems provide us with an adequate image of students in educational relationships. And when I tried to imagine what intelligent adaptive systems look like, the robot vacuum cleaner was the first image that came to my mind. And perhaps it came to my mind because in French, these machines are known as 'aspirateurs autonome'—and it was the word 'autonome' that captured my attention as an educationalist. So what do robot vacuum cleaners reveal about the prevailing educational imaginary?

What is interesting about robot vacuum cleaners is, first of all, that they are indeed able to perform their task—hoovering a room—autonomously. But what perhaps is even more interesting is that over time, they can become more efficient at doing so, because they can adapt—intelligently—to the particular room in which they have to perform their task. If their pattern is at first rather random or, to be more precise, guided by the particular algorithm they were programmed with, over time it becomes more adjusted to the situation in which they have to perform their task. We can say, therefore, that robot vacuum cleaners can *learn* or, if we wish, we can say that they can adapt to their environment in an intelligent way. While their learning is autonomous, it does not mean that it cannot be influenced. The way to do it, the way to let them learn more and different things, is by putting the machine in a different environment so that it needs to adapt to differing environing conditions. One can even assume that robot vacuum cleaners which have adjusted to a range of different rooms become more effective at adapting to any new room they are placed in. While their learning remains a lifelong task—each new situation may pose new challenges and thus will require further (intelligent) adaptation—they may nonetheless become more skilled at adapting to new situations.

I believe that the foregoing account provides a fairly accurate picture of *a*, and perhaps even *the* prevailing contemporary educational imaginary. This is an imaginary that sees education as a learner-centred endeavour, where it is ultimately for learners to construct their own understandings and build their own skills, and where the main task of teachers is to provide arrangements in and through which such processes can happen. In this situation, the teacher does, indeed, no longer transmit anything, but designs learning environments for students in order to facilitate their learning.

LEVINAS AND THE PHILOSOPHY OF EDUCATION

Similarly, students are not engaged in passive absorption but in active adaptive construction, and it is through this that they acquire the skills and competences that make them more able to adapt to future situations. This also shifts the meaning and position of the curriculum, which no longer exists as the content to be transmitted and acquired, but becomes redefined as a set of 'learning opportunities' in and through which students, in a flexible and personalised way, pursue their own 'learning lines' (a concept that has become popular in the design of school education in the Netherlands, see http://nl.wikipedia.org/wiki/Leerlijn).

It is perhaps important to note that while this imaginary is contemporary—by which I seek to say that it is shaping contemporary educational practice in many contexts and settings—its theoretical frame is not new. We can find it, for example in the theory of autopoietic systems, that is, of systems that are able to regenerate themselves in constant interaction with their environment—an idea that was developed in biology by Humberto Maturana and Francis Varela (see, e.g. Maturana & Varela, 1980; Varela, Maturana, & Uribe, 1974) and that was further developed by Niklas Luhmann in his theory of social systems (Luhmann, 1984, 1995). Here, we can indeed find the idea that such systems (e.g. human individuals) cannot participate in each other's autopoiesis—which for example can mean that they cannot participate in each other's adaptive activities or cognitive constructions—but that they can interfere in each other's environments so as to have an indirect effect on each other's autopoiesis. But perhaps the most famous example of the frame underlying the ideas outlined above can be found in the work of John Dewey, whose understanding of action, communication and learning is based on a view of the human organism as being in ongoing transaction with its (natural and social) environment, constantly seeking to establish a dynamic equilibrium in processes of doing and undergoing (see Dewey, 1925). And in Dewey, we can indeed also find the claim that 'we never educate directly, but indirectly by means of the environment' (Dewey, 1966/1916, p. 19).

If I were to characterise the underlying anthropology—that is, the view about the human being and its place in the world—I would suggest to call this a hermeneutical anthropology and, more widely, a hermeneutical world view. The reason for using these phrases is that the human being appears here first and foremost as a sense-making being, that is, as a being who is in relationship with the world—natural and social—through acts of interpretation and comprehension. Such acts are issued from the self and, 'via' the world so to speak, return to the self. They are acts of comprehension in the literal sense of the word, in that they try to grasp ('pre-hendere') the world in its totality ('com'). In such acts of comprehension, in such hermeneutical acts, the world thus appears as an object of our sense-making, our understanding and interpretation. One could—simply and straightforwardly—say that this is indeed the case. One could, in other words, affirm that the hermeneutical world view is *true*, and that we should therefore build our understanding of knowledge and communication, but also of ethics, politics and education upon this premise.[4] But one could also pause for a moment and ponder whether the hermeneutical world view is as inevitable as it would seem, perhaps by asking what is *not* conceivable within the confines of this world view.

There are two issues that I would like to mention here. One is the question whether in the hermeneutical world view the world, natural and social, *can speak* in its own terms and on its own terms. The second is whether in the hermeneutical world view we can be *spoken to*, that is, whether we can be addressed (see also Biesta, 2012b). The hermeneutical world view, so I wish to suggest, precisely seems to preclude these two options (and it is important, as I will try to make clear below, to see them as two *different* limitations of the hermeneutical world view). The reason for this lies in the fact that the hermeneutical world view depicts a universe that is *immanent* to my understanding, to acts of my comprehension that always aim to bring the world 'out there' back to me. While such acts of comprehension do have an object—hermeneutics is not phantasy or pure construction—this object always appears as an object of *my* signification and, in this sense, remains dependent on these acts of *signification*. In the next two sections, I take up these two aspects—the question of immanence and the question of signification—in conversation with two texts from Levinas.

'An opening in an opening': On Signification and Sense

In his article, 'Signification and Sense' (Levinas, 2006; a different English translation was called 'Meaning and Sense', see Levinas, 2008; the original French version was published in 1964), Levinas explores both the limitations and the conditions of possibility of signification, broadly conceived as (acts of) meaning making. One line in the complex and rich argument Levinas puts forward concerns what he refers to as the 'anti-Platonism in contemporary philosophy of signification' (Levinas, 2006, p. 18). This anti-Platonism, which he sees in Hegelian, Bergsonian and phenomenological philosophies of signification, concerns the contention that, as he puts it, 'the intelligible is inconceivable outside the becoming that suggests it' (Levinas, 2006, p. 18). It is the idea that '(t) here does not exist any *signification in itself* that a thought could reach by hopping over the reflections—distorting or faithful, but sensible—that lead to it' (Levinas, 2006, p. 18; emph. in original). Or in slightly more concrete language, it is the idea that '(a)ll things picturesque, all the different cultures, are no longer obstacles that separate us from the essential and the Intelligible (but are) the only possible paths, irreplaceable, and consequently implicated in the intelligible itself' (Levinas, 2006, p. 18).

Levinas thus describes a situation of total *immanence*—all our meaning making, all our signification, occurs 'inside' culture and history—which he characterises as anti-Platonic because, as he writes, for Plato 'the world of significations *precedes* the language and culture that express it' so that it remains 'indifferent to the system of signs that can be invented to make this world present to thought' (Levinas, 2006, p. 18) Plato, so Levinas argues, believed in the existence of 'a privileged culture (that) can understand the transitory and seemingly childish nature of historical cultures' (Levinas, 2006, pp. 18–19); a privileged culture that, so we might say, could give sense *to* signification and make sense *of* signification. Levinas shows that in contemporary philosophy of signification this option is no longer considered to be possible. What we find instead is a '*subordination* of intellect to expression' (Levinas, 2006, p. 19; emphasis added).

LEVINAS AND THE PHILOSOPHY OF EDUCATION

For Levinas, this not only poses a *philosophical* problem—which I have alluded to as the question where signification gets its meaning or sense from (I will return to this below). It also poses a *practical* problem that has to do with the (im)possibility of communication (to which I will return below as well). And it poses an urgent *political* problem, because this 'most recent, most daring and influential anthropology keeps multiple cultures on the same level' (Levinas, 2006, p. 20). According to Levinas's analysis, the contemporary philosophy of signification thus amounts to cultural and historical relativism. Because of its total immanence, it lacks a criterion that would make any judgement about acts of signification (and wider practices and cultures of signification) possible so as to distinguish between those that 'make sense' and those that do not 'make sense'. Without such a criterion, all significations and all systems and cultures of signification are simply 'there'—on the same level. As this is clearly an undesirable situation for Levinas, he raises the question where such a criterion might come from.

One option Levinas briefly discusses is the suggestion that human need can provide such a criterion. The idea here is that '(n)eed raises things simply given to the rank of values', that '(m)an confers a unique sense to being by working it', so that '(i)n scientific technical culture the ambiguity of being, like the ambiguity of signification, is surmounted' (Levinas, 2006, p. 21). Yet Levinas does not consider this 'materialism'—to which he also refers as 'economic signification' (see Levinas, 2006)—to be a viable option, because, unlike what its proponents claim, the 'technical designation of the universe' has itself to be seen as another 'modality of culture' and not as something that transcends culture (Levinas, 2006).[5] Does that mean that we can do nothing more than celebrate plurality? This is indeed what Levinas observes in 'contemporary philosophy' in that it simply 'takes satisfaction [*se complait*] in the multiplicity of cultural significations' (Levinas, 2006, pp. 25–26). In his analysis, this manifests itself as a 'refusal of engagement in the Other' (Levinas, 2006, p. 26). Yet it is precisely in the latter movement that Levinas sees an opening.

There are two aspects to how Levinas constructs his argument here, and along both lines, he seeks to establish that signification 'is situated before Culture' and that it is 'situated in Ethics (which is the) presupposition of all Culture and all signification' (Levinas, 2006, p. 36).[6] Rather than to refuse engagement in the Other, it is precisely this engagement which, according to Levinas, is the origin of sense in that it provides an 'orientation' (Levinas, 2006, p. 26). In a first step, Levinas characterises this orientation 'as a motion from the identical toward an Other that is absolutely other' (Levinas, 2006, p. 26). This orientation which, as Levinas puts it, 'goes freely from Same to Other' is what he refers to as 'a Work' (Levinas, 2006, p. 26; capitals in original). But for the Work to be radically Other-centred, it 'must not be thought as an apparent agitation of a stock that afterward remains identical to itself', nor must it be thought 'as similar to the technique that ... transforms a strange world into a world whose otherness is converted to my idea' (Levinas, 2006, p. 26)—which I read as another definition of the hermeneutical 'gesture'. Hence, the Work needs to be understood as '*a movement of the Same toward the Other that never returns to the Same*' (Levinas, 2006, p. 26, emphasis in original).

This line of thinking, which is akin to Derrida's analysis of the gift (see, e.g. Derrida, 1992, 1995), leads Levinas to such observations as that the Work not only requires 'a radical generosity of movement' but that, because of this, it also demands *'ingratitude* from the Other', in that the other is not supposed to 'return' the Work by being grateful for it, as this would bring the Work back into a circle of economic calculation of costs and benefits, of expenses and returns (Levinas, 2006, pp. 26–27). Levinas writes: 'As absolute orientation toward the Other—as sense—the work is possible only in the patience that, pushed to the limit, signifies that the Agent renounces contemporaneity with its fulfilment, that he acts without entering the Promised Land' (Levinas, 2006, p. 27). The word that Levinas eventually suggests for this work is *liturgy* which 'in its first signification means the exercise of an office that is not only totally gratuitous but requires from the executant an investment at a loss'—and it is this 'uncompensated work' which Levinas names as 'ethics itself' (Levinas, 2006, p. 28).[7]

Liturgy, Need and Desire

To keep liturgy—or in a more complex formulation: 'sense as the liturgical orientation of the work' (Levinas, 2006, p. 29)—away from need, Levinas introduces the notion of desire (see Levinas, 2006, p. 39). Here, desire is not to be understood as a desire for fulfilment, which is why Levinas writes that '(t)he Desire for Others—sociality—arises in a being who lacks nothing or, more exactly, arises beyond all that could be lacking or satisfying to him' (Levinas, 2006). In desire, the ego goes out to the Other 'in a way that compromises the sovereign identification of the Ego with oneself' (Levinas, 2006). But how should we 'approach' this 'Desire for Others that', according to Levinas, 'we feel in the most common social experience' (Levinas, 2006, p. 30). Levinas observes that '(a)ll analysis of language in contemporary philosophy emphasises, and rightfully so, its hermeneutic structure' (Levinas, 2006, p. 30), that is, that our approach to the other is to be understood as an act of signification. Yet Levinas is after a 'third option' where the other is neither 'collaborator and neighbour of our cultural work of expression [nor] client of our artistic production, but *interlocutor*; the one to whom expression expresses' (Levinas, 2006, p. 30, emphasis added). Precisely here we find a first and crucial 'opening', in that Levinas suggests that signification is not an egological act, it is not a gesture through which the ego generates meaning, it is not self-generated expression 'onto' a world (hermeneutics) because 'before it is a celebration of being, expression is a relation with the one to whom I express the expression' (Levinas, 2006, p. 30).

This Other 'who faces me' is precisely for this reason 'not included in the totality of being that is expressed'—because in that case, the other would be the 'product' of my signification—but arises 'behind all collection of being, as the one to whom I express what I express' (Levinas, 2006, p. 30). This is so because it is only through the (presence of the) Other as *interlocutor* that 'a phenomenon such as signification [can] introduce itself, of itself, into being' (Levinas, 2006, p. 30). That is why, as interlocutor, as the one to whom I express the expression 'and whose presence is already required so that my cultural gesture of expression can be produced', the Other is 'neither a cultural signification nor a simple given' but rather 'primordially, *sense*' (Levinas, 2006, p. 30, emphasis in original). And here we have to remember that 'sense' for Levinas is precisely that which gives our signification meaning and, going on from this, gives our life direction. Levinas emphasises that this 'turn'—about I wish to say one more thing below—'means returning in a new way to Platonism' (Levinas, 2006, p. 38) because it allows to go beyond 'this saraband of countless equivalent cultures, each one justifying itself in its own context' (Levinas, 2006, p. 37). While Levinas praises Husserl for a similar achievement that would (again) allow 'for ethical judgements about civilizations' (Levinas, 2006, p. 37), he notes that '(o)ne is not obliged to follow the same path Husserl took', which was that of 'postulating phenomenological reduction and constitution ... of the cultural world in the intuitive transcendental consciousness' (Levinas, 2006, p. 37). Levinas claims that he has found a different avenue towards 'the rectitude of signification', namely through the idea that 'intelligible manifestation is produced in the rectitude of *morality* and in the Work'—understood as liturgy (Levinas, 2006, p. 37, emphasis added).

Before I draw this section to a conclusion, there is one more aspect of Levinas's line of thought that needs to be brought in, a line which responds to the point raised above about the (im)possibility of communication or interlocution. This, in simple terms, has to do with the question how the Other—in English translation always with a capital 'O'—can be interlocutor. It is here that a second opening takes place. While Levinas acknowledges that the manifestation of the Other—and the word manifestation should be taken literally, that is, the way in which the Other manifests itself—'is of course produced ... in the way all signification is produced', that is, through an action of my 'comprehension of the Other' which, as Levinas emphasises, is 'a hermeneutic, an exegesis' (Levinas, 2006, pp. 30–31), the Other does not only come to us through manifestation, that is, as a 'product' of our signification.

If that were the case, then signification would remain the original event even if this signification would have an ethical quality, for example coming from my intention to want to do good to the other or care for the other. In addition to the manifestation of the other, that is, in addition to the appearance of the Other as *phenomenon*, there is also the 'epiphany of the Other'—an epiphany that bears its own significance, 'independent of the signification received from the world' (Levinas, 2006, p. 31). The Other 'not only comes to us from a context but signifies itself, without that mediation' (Levinas, 2006, p. 31)—and it is this unmediated presence coming to us to which Levinas refers as 'face' and it is to the epiphany of the face that Levinas refers as 'visitation' (see Levinas, 2006, p. 31). Face, so we might say, 'breaks through' its signification, that is, through its image. This is a process of 'deformalization' (Cohen, 2006, p. xxxi) where the face speaks and where this speaking 'is first and foremost this way of coming from behind one's appearance, behind one's form; an opening in the opening' (Levinas, 2006, p. 31).

But the face does not speak in general—its speaking is not 'the unveiling of the world' (Levinas, 2006, p. 31).[8] Rather the face speaks to *me*; the face addresses me, the face summons me and 'announces thereby the ethical dimensions of visitation' (Levinas, 2006, p. 32). It is precisely here that '(c)onsciousness loses its first place' (Levinas, 2006, p. 32) because 'the presence of the face signifies an irrefutable order —a commandment—that arrests the availability of consciousness' (Levinas, 2006, p. 32). Levinas emphasises that in this moment, consciousness is challenged by the

LEVINAS AND THE PHILOSOPHY OF EDUCATION

face, but that it is crucial to see that this challenge 'does not come from awareness of that challenge' (Levinas, 2006, p. 32) because in that case, signification would come before the address. 'This is a challenge of consciousness, not a consciousness of the challenge' (Levinas, 2006, p. 33). This visitation is therefore 'the upset of the very egoism of the Ego' (Levinas, 2006, p. 33). It is important to see, however, that this does not amount to the destruction of the Ego but rather to what we might call a decentring; a decentring through which the 'Me/Ego' gains its unique significance. As Levinas explains, the responsibility 'that empties the Ego of its imperialism [rather] confirms the uniqueness of the Ego', a uniqueness which lies in the fact 'that no one can answer in my stead' (Levinas, 2006, p. 33). And discovering 'such an orientation for the Ego means identifying Ego and morality' (Levinas, 2006, p. 33)—and hence the moral 'origin' of the Ego-as-subject (hence the idea of an ethics of subjectivity mentioned above).

Revelation, Transcendence and Ethics

I have followed Levinas's argument in much detail in order to show how this single (and singular) line of thought addresses the problems stemming from what Levinas refers to as the contemporary philosophy of signification. These problems were the question of *sense*—Where does signification get its meaning from?—the question of *communication*—How is communication possible in a radically plural universe?—and the question of the *criterion*—What makes it possible for us to evaluate (systems and traditions of) signification? Levinas's line of thought provides an answer to these three questions, not so much to each of the questions separately, but more in an overlapping and interlocking way. One key insight is the observation that signification is not an egological act or accomplishment, but consists of a relation with the one to whom I express an expression, the one to whom expression expresses. Signification thus derives its sense from this particular 'event'. In this relation, the Other does not appear as object of my signification, but as interlocutor. That is why the 'appearance' of the Other is not a matter of manifestation—the other is not a phenomenon—but of epiphany. What appears, therefore, is not an image of the Other, but what Levinas refers to as its face.

It is important to see that the face does not thematise me; the face does not make me into an object of its signification. Rather the face speaks to me. Yet this speech—and this is crucial as well—is not a revelation of the Other that I am just to receive.[9] The key idea here is that the face speaks to *me* or, to be more precise: the speech of the face addresses me (and here we need to emphasise both the fact that the face *addresses* and that the face addresses *me*, in the singular, and not just anyone). It is an address in which my imperialism is interrupted, where my consciousness is challenged —'(t)he face disorients the intentionality that sights it' (see Biesta, 2012b; Levinas, 2006, p. 33)—where I am summoned to respond. And it is in this moment, in this ethical event, that the Ego gains its significance, precisely because it appears beyond/before/outside of any signification. In short, then, the 'criterion' Levinas identifies is ethics; communication is a matter of being spoken to, of being addressed; and it is in the ethical event of being addressed that signification acquires its sense, that signification first becomes possible—or with a more precise formulation from Levinas: that signification introduces itself into being.

Before I return to the question of teaching with which I have started this article, I wish to look briefly at another short text from Levinas called 'Revelation in the Jewish Tradition' (Levinas, 1989; originally published in French in 1977). In this text, Levinas also provides a critique of the hermeneutical world view, but in a slightly different register and vocabulary. Some might say that the text is radically different rather than slightly different as it deals with a theological question of the possibility of revelation. I see more continuity between this question and the themes of 'Signification and Sense', as in both cases, Levinas is trying to articulate a critique of immanence (see also Biesta, 2013a), and it is on this aspect that my reading here will focus. That the main 'theme' is the overcoming of immanence, is already clear in the opening sentence where Levinas states that the 'fundamental question' he is addressing 'is less concerned with the content attributed to revelation than with the actual fact—a metaphysical one—referred to as the Revelation' (Levinas, 1989, p. 191). Levinas goes even one step further by arguing that this fact in itself is 'the first content, and the most important, to be revealed by any revelation' (Levinas, 1989, p. 191). The 'point' of revelation is its exteriority—that revelation is something that comes to us from the outside. Hence, the question how we can 'make sense of the "exteriority" of the truths and signs of the Revelation which strike the human faculty known as reason' (Levinas, 1989, p. 192). '(H)ow can these truths and signs strike our reason if they are not even of this world?'

Part of the answer to this question is given in the idea of 'the reader's participation in the Revelation' (Levinas, 1989, p. 194). While this may, at first sight, sound like an argument for interpretation that would bring hermeneutics back to the scene—and there are parts of the text where Levinas does indeed create space for hermeneutics; where it is also important to note that Levinas does not deny signification but seeks to decentre it—Levinas does not reduce revelation to hermeneutics but has a rather different relationship between revelation and the self in mind. He writes that while 'its word comes from elsewhere, from outside [it lives at the same time] within the person receiving it' (Levinas, 1989, p. 194). Levinas claims therefore that the only '"terrain" where exteriority can appear is in the human being' (Levinas, 1989, p. 194). But the human being here 'does far more than listen' (Levinas, 1989, p. 194). That Levinas does not understand this in terms of hermeneutics becomes clear when he argues that the message that comes from the outside does not come 'in order to collide with a reason which is "free"' but rather arrives 'to assume instead a unique shape, which cannot be reduced to a contingent "subjective impression"' (Levinas, 1989, pp. 194–195). Rather '(t)he Revelation has a particular way of producing meaning, which lies in its calling upon the unique within me' (Levinas, 1989, p. 195). Revelation, in the language from the previous section, speaks to me or, to be more precise: addresses me, calls me, summons me.

That is why, in a familiar line, Levinas emphasises that '(m)y very uniqueness lies in my responsibility for the other [in the sense that] nobody can relieve me of this, just as nobody can replace me at the moment of my death' (Levinas, 1989, p. 202). This allows Levinas to articulate a very different notion of freedom—not the liberal freedom of being able to do what one wishes to do, but being free as 'simply [doing] what nobody else can do in my place' so that 'to be free' means 'to obey the Most High' (Levinas, 1989, p. 202). Just as God interrupts the human being, Levinas highlights that 'man is also the interruption of God within Being, or the bursting out of Being towards God' (Levinas, 1989, p. 202). 'Man is the fracture in Being which produces the act of giving, with hands which are full, in place of fighting and pillaging' (Levinas, 1989, p. 202). Levinas explains that this is where the idea of being chosen comes from. He acknowledges that this idea can 'deteriorate in pride, but originally expresses the awareness of an appointment which cannot be called into question; an appointment which is the basis of ethics and which ... isolates the person in its responsibility' (Levinas, 1989, p. 202).

This brings Levinas back to the idea of subjectivity as 'the very fracturing of immanence' (Levinas, 1989, p. 204). But how can this fracturing be understood? We might say that understanding is precisely the way in which this fracturing cannot be understood because if the fracturing, that which comes from the outside, is 'thinkable' then it is already, via a hermeneutical gesture, made 'safe', that is, it no longer is a fracturing. Levinas observes that the difficulty here 'stems from our habit of thinking of reason as the correlative of the possibility of the world, the counterpart to its stability and identity' (Levinas, 1989, p. 205). Could it be otherwise, he asks? 'Could we account for intelligibility in terms of a traumatic upheaval in experience, which confronts intelligence with something far beyond its capacity, and thereby causes it to break?' (Levinas, 1989, p. 205).

As long as we think of the whole process of revelation as the revelation of a truth to reason, then all this does not really make sense. But Levinas sees an entirely different option, the one where 'we consider the possibility of a command, a "you must," which takes no account of what "you can."' (Levinas, 1989, p. 205). In this case, Levinas argues, 'the exceeding of one's capacity does make sense' because the type of reason corresponding to the fracture 'is practical reason' (Levinas, 1989, p. 205) which must mean, so Levinas concludes, that 'our model of revelation be an ethical one' (Levinas, 1989, p. 206). Here, notions such as 'prescription' and 'obedience' play a role (see Levinas, 1989, p. 206). But the obedience Levinas has in mind 'cannot be assimilated to the categorical imperative, where a universal suddenly finds itself in a position to direct the will' (Levinas, 1989, p. 206). It rather derives 'from the love of one's neighbour, a love without eros, lacking self-indulgence, which is, in this sense, a love that is obeyed' (Levinas, 1989, p. 206).

This 'love that is obeyed' hints at the possibility 'of a heteronomy which does not involve servitude, a receptive ear which still retains its reason, an obedience which does not alienate the person listening' so as to be able to recognise what Levinas refers to as 'the transcendence of understanding' (Levinas, 1989, p. 207). Levinas is aware that 'such moves towards acknowledging an irreducible transcendence' cannot occur within 'the dominant conception of reason held by the philosophical profession today'—by which he has in mind what elsewhere in this article I have referred to as the hermeneutical world view which starts from the self and conceives of the self's relationship with the word in terms of sense-making. 'Nothing can fissure the nuclear solidity of this power of thought', Levinas writes, 'a thought which freezes its object as a theme' (Levinas, 1989, p. 207). This is different from the ethical relationship with the Other which, 'unlike the exteriority which surrounds man whenever he seeks knowledge ... cannot be transformed into a content within interiority [but] remains "uncontainable" [while] the relation is maintained' (Levinas, 1989, p. 207). Hence, Levinas's solution for the 'paradox of revelation' is one that claims that we may find a model for this relation with exteriority 'in the attitude of non-indifference towards the Other (...) and that it is precisely through this relation that man becomes his "self"' (Levinas, 1989, p. 207). Ethics, then, 'provides the model worthy of transcendence' (Levinas, 1989, p. 207), one where 'the Same—drowsy in his identity' is *awakened* by the Other (Levinas, 1989, p. 207).[10]

On the Rediscovery of Teaching

I started this article with some critical questions about the all too common and all too facile critique of traditional teaching—a critique that seems to have become the new dogma of contemporary educational thought. I showed how this critique has led to a demise of teaching and the teacher and a turn towards learning; a turn where the teacher can only exist as a facilitator of otherwise autonomous learning processes. From the 'sage on the stage', the teacher seems to have become the 'guide on the side' and, according to some, even the 'peer at the rear'. The reason for the emergence of the turn towards learning seems to lie in the fact that 'traditional' teaching is perceived as an act of *control.* That this is so also becomes visible when we look at the motivation of those who, in light of the turn towards learning, are making a case in favour of teaching, because they do so precisely because they want teaching to be a powerful act of control aimed at maintaining or restoring individual and societal order. While order is not necessarily bad—the question is not whether or not we need order, but when and where we need what kind of order and for what purposes; think, for example of the immense importance of the legal order—the problem with the idea of teaching as control is *that in such a relationship the student can never appear as a subject,* but remains an object. In a world that is not interested in the subjectness of the human being this is, of course, not a problem. The question is whether this is a world we should desire.[11]

Yet what emerges from the ideas put forward in this article is that the option that is a proposed response to the idea of teaching-as-control, namely the idea of learning and, more specifically that of learning-as-meaning-making (signification) and of the learner as a meaning maker, suffers from the same problem in that, again, in acts of meaning making *the learner also cannot appear as a subject.* One way to understand why this is so has to do with the fact that the act of signification is issued from the self and returns—'via' the world as I have put it—to the self. Signification thus keeps the self to the self—never interrupted, always already identical with itself and sufficient for itself. Another way of looking at it is to say that in its ongoing attempts to adapt and adjust to changing environing conditions the self remains an object vis-à-vis the environment it is adapting and adjusting itself to. While this may help the self to *survive*—and it is remarkable how much of contemporary educational discourse is about survival, for example with regard to the apparent skills, students need to survive in an unknown future—it never creates a possibility for the self to *exist* (also in the literal sense of being outside of itself). The question that never arises, to put it differently, is whether the environment to which the self is adapting and adjusting is *good* in the fullest sense of that world. To put it differently: the self—and perhaps we should say the adjusting self or the hermeneutical self—can never out of its own generate a criterion with which to evaluate that which it is adjusting to. It is thus 'caught', as an object, in that which it is adjusting to, an issue that is particularly visible in the image of the robot vacuum cleaner.

This is where the 'opening' Levinas creates through his critique of the hermeneutical world view has its significance, as he shows that our subjectness is not constituted from the 'inside' through acts of interpretation and adaptation, but is called into being from the outside, as an interruption of my immanence, an interruption or fracturing of my being-with-myself, of my consciousness. This is neither the moment where I interpret the other, nor the moment where I listen to the other (see Biesta, 2012b), nor is it the moment where the other makes sense of me—it is, in this regard, outside of the realm of signification. It rather is *the moment where I am addressed* by the other, where the other, in Levinas's words, '[calls] upon the unique within me'. *And may not this event of being addressed give us an entirely different and far more significant account of teaching and the experience of being taught?*[12]

It is in light of this that we can begin to see why the idea of intelligent adaptive systems such as robot vacuum cleaners precisely does *not* provide us with an adequate image of students in educational relationships. While, as mentioned, such systems can learn, can adapt and adjust to their environments, and can, in this regard, be said to be capable of signification, the very 'thing' that cannot happen, the very 'thing' that can never 'arrive' in their universe, is the event of being addressed, that is, the event of being taught. In short, then, while such systems can learn, they cannot be taught.

Here, then do we encounter an altogether different 'account' of the event of teaching, one that is precisely *not* aimed at control, at the exercise of power and the establishment of an order in which the student can only exist as object, but rather one that calls forth the subjectness of the student by interrupting its egocentrism, its being-with-itself and for-itself. This is not only a teaching that puts us very differently in the world (and in this regard it can be seen as teaching with existential import). We could even say that this teaching puts us in the world in the first place. It is (a) teaching that draws us out of ourselves, as it interrupts our 'needs', to use Levinas's term, or, in the vocabulary, I have introduced elsewhere (Biesta, 2014), as it interrupts our desires, and in this sense, frees us from the ways in which we are bound to or even determined by our desires. It does so by introducing the question whether what we desire is actually desirable, both for ourselves and for the life we live with what and who is other.

Such teaching is not authoritarian—it does not reduce the student to an object but rather has an interest in the student's subjectness. But it does not overcome authoritarianism by *opposing* it (which would mean leaving students entirely to their own devices, that is, to their own learning-as-signification). It does so by establishing an entirely different relationship. This is a relationship of authority—bearing in mind that authority *is* relational (Bingham, 2008)—because in moving from what we desire to what we can consider desirable, we give authority to what and who is other or, with a slightly different word, we *authorise* what and who is other by letting it be an author, that is, a subject who speaks and addresses us.

We have arrived, then, at the option that seems to be absent in the current way in which the critique of traditional teaching is being conducted, namely where the critique of teaching-as-control immediately ends up with the idea of learning as freedom. In the preceding pages, I have not only tried to argue that a different alternative *is* possible. I have also suggested that a different alternative *ought to be* possible because if we replace teaching-as-control with an alleged freedom of signification, we actually reinforce the student's unfreedom because, as I have tried to make clear through my discussion of Levinas, the student remains with himself or herself and, in acts of signification, always returns to himself or herself, but never comes into the world, never achieves its subjectness.

These ideas begin to outline a non-egological approach to education, an approach that is not aimed at strengthening the ego, but at interrupting the *ego-object*—turning it towards the world, perhaps even pulling it into the world (see Mollenhauer, 2014) —so that it can become a *self-subject*. Here, the quote from Philippe Meirieu which is at the start of this article has its meaning, as it suggests that what education should aim for is for the 'student-subject' to be in the world—rather than remain with itself —without being or becoming the centre of the world. Being in the world without being the centre of the world, that is, being in the world without trying, in a rather infantile way, to control the world, means to be or exist in the world in a *grown up* way, that is, in a subject–subject relationship, rather than a subject–object relationship in which the world can only appear as an object of my signification, of my needs. It is a way of being in the world where I have not become immune for what seeks to address me—a way of being in the world, in short, where I can be taught.

Acknowledgment

I would like to thank Guoping Zhao for her invitation to contribute to this special issue and for her generous feedback on an earlier version of this article. I would also like to thank Vanessa de Oliveira Andreotti and Wouter Pols for their encouragement to pursue the ideas in this article.

Disclosure statement

No potential conflict of interest was reported by the author.

Notes

1. I refer here to philosophical anthropology, not empirical or 'cultural' anthropology.
2. I prefer the notion of 'subjectness' over that of 'subjectivity' as the latter has echoes of subjectivity as the opposite of objectivity, whereas what I seek to refer to is the 'condition' of being a subject rather than an object.
3. In a forthcoming article, Zhao (in press) has raised some questions about my existential reading of Levinas's approach to the question of human subjectness. She does this in the context of the discussion about humanism. I take (philosophical) humanism as any attempt to articulate a truth about the human subject, whether such a truth sees the subject as fixed and self-enclosed, or as open, intersubjective and always in the making. The problem with

humanism is therefore not about the particular conception of the human subject—in which case the challenge would only be to come up with a better conception—but about the very idea that it is possible and desirable for the subject to jump over its own shadow in order to define itself, be it as fixed or be it as open. I see this, and not a concern about a particular conception of the human being, as the main thrust of the critique of humanism in Heidegger, Levinas and Foucault. What I value in Levinas is that he approaches the question of human subjectness not through a theory about the subject, but through the articulation of an event where my subjectness—as a first person issue and not a third person account—is 'at stake'. In my work, I have particularly been interested in exploring humanist challenges and post-humanist possibilities for education—and this exploration is ongoing.

4. I am inclined to say that pragmatism—particularly in the work of Dewey and Mead—provides one of the most developed examples of this 'programme'. This article can therefore also be read as an exploration of the limits of the pragmatic world view and everything that has emerged from this world view, including a theory and practice of education.

5. I raise this issue because, despite its philosophical sophistication, I believe that pragmatism basically starts from an anthropology of human need and, in this regard, retains a technical orientation towards the world, albeit one that is acutely aware of the moral and political challenges of such an orientation.

6. It is, therefore, the manifestation of the ethical event—or to be (much) more precise: the epiphany of the ethical demand—that gives sense to signification. This is discussed in more detail in what follows.

7. It might be interesting to ponder the extent to which teaching can be understood according to Levinas's conception of liturgy.

8. I take this as a critique of Heidegger's notion of *aletheia*—truth as unveiling.

9. I do not have the space in this article to engage in detail with the distance between Levinas and Heidegger, but this is one point where this distance appears and where, in my view, Levinas crucially moves beyond Heidegger. Whereas, to put it briefly and crudely, Heidegger and Levinas both see a similar problem with signification—namely that signification is egological, that it is driven by the self and always returns to the self—Heidegger proposes that the alternative to signification is reception, where we receive what speaks to us and care for it, whereas Levinas proposes that the alternative to self-enclosed signification lies in the fact that what speaks to us addresses us, singles us out, and summons a response. Whereas pure receptivity is ultimately criterion-less—it has no criterion to 'select' or judge what it should care for—Levinas 'moves' us from receptivity to responsibility, where the question for me is not how to receive and hold, but to ask what is being asked from me (with the emphasis, once more, on me in the singular, not on anyone in general). The distance between Heidegger and Levinas is also the reason why, earlier in this article, I identified two different problems with the hermeneutical world view—not only the problem how the world can speak in its own terms, but also how we can be spoken to.

10. It might also be interesting to ponder the extent to which teaching might be seen as a process of awakening.

11. I formulate this as a relatively open question in order to highlight the normative reference point in my discussion. Nonetheless the twentieth century in particular has shown the devastating consequences of totalitarian world views which precisely are not interested in the subjectness of the human being—or reserve the right to subjectness only to a privileged selection.

12. I make the distinction between 'teaching' and 'being taught' because a difficult but important issue in this discussion has to do with the question whether the teacher has the power to teach or whether the event of being taught should be understood as a gift that neither can be fully given by the teacher nor enforced by the student, but may nonetheless arrive in educational relationships (I discuss this in more detail in Biesta 2013a. I also refer the reader to Zhao (2014) for a probing discussion of these ideas.

ORCID

Gert Biesta ⓘ http://orcid.org/0000-0001-8530-7105

References

Bauman, Z. (1993). *Postmodern ethics*. Oxford: Wiley-Blackwell.

Biesta, G. J. J. (2008). Pedagogy with empty hands: Levinas, education and the question of being human. In D. Egéa-Kuehne (Ed.), *Levinas and education: At the intersection of faith and reason* (pp. 198–210). London: Routledge.

Biesta, G. J. J. (2010). *Good education in an age of measurement: Ethics, politics, democracy*. Boulder, CO: Paradigm Publishers.

Biesta, G. J. J. (2012a). Giving teaching back to education. Responding to the disappearance of the teacher. *Phenomenology and Practice, 6,* 35–49.

Biesta, G. J. J. (2012b). No education without hesitation. Thinking differently about educational relations. In C. Ruitenberg (Ed.), *Philosophy of education 2012* (pp. 1–13). Urbana-Champaign, IL: PES.

Biesta, G. J. J. (2013a). Receiving the gift of teaching: From 'learning from' to 'being taught by'. *Studies in Philosophy and Education, 32,* 449–461.

Biesta, G. J. J. (2013b). Interrupting the politics of learning. *Power and Education, 5*(1), 4–15.

Biesta, G. J. J. (2014). *The beautiful risk of education*. Boulder, CO: Paradigm Publishers.

Biesta, G. J. J., & Stengel, B. (in press). Thinking philosophically about teaching: Illuminating issues and (re)framing research. In D. Gittomer & C. Bell (Eds.), *AREA handbook of research on teaching* (5th ed.). Washington, DC: AERA.

Bingham, C. (2008). *Authority is relational*. Albany, NY: SUNY Press.

Cohen, R. A. (2006). Introduction. In E. Levinas (Ed.), *Humanism of the other* (pp. vii–xliv). Urbana, IL: Illinois University Press.

Derrida, J. (1992). *Given time: I counterfeit money*. Chicago, IL: University of Chicago Press.

Derrida, J. (1995). *The gift of death*. Chicago, IL: University of Chicago Press.

Dewey, J. (1925). Experience and nature. In J. A. Boydston (Ed.), *John Dewey. The later works (1925–1953)* (Vol. 1). Carbondale, IL: Southern Illinois University Press.

Dewey, J. (1966/1916). *Democracy and education*. New York, NY: The Free Press.

Levinas, E. (1985). *Ethics and infinity. Conversations with Philippe Nemo*. Pittsburgh, PA: Duquesne University Press.

Levinas, E. (1989). Revelation in the Jewish tradition. In S. Hand (Ed.), *The Levinas reader* (pp. 190–210). Oxford: Blackwell.

Levinas, E. (1994). *Outside the subject*. Stanford, CA: Stanford University Press.

Levinas, E. (2006). *Humanism of the other*. Urbana, IL: Illinois University Press.

Levinas, E. (2008). Meaning and sense. In A. T. Peperzak, S. Critchley, & R. Bernasconi (Eds.), *Emmanuel Levinas: Basic philosophical writings* (pp. 33–64). Bloomington, IN: Indiana University Press.

Luhmann, N. (1995). *Social systems*. Stanford, CA: Stanford University Press.

Luhmann, N. (1984). *Soziale Systeme: Grundriß einer allgemeinen Theorie* [Social systems: Outline of a general theory]. Frankfurt am Main: Suhrkamp.

Maturana, H. R., & Varela, F. J. (1980). *Autopoiesis and cognition: The realization of the living.* Dordrecht: D. Reidel Publishing Company.

Meirieu, P. (2007). *Pédagogie: Le devoir de résister* [Education: The duty to resist]. Issy-les-Moulineaux: ESF éditeur.

Mollenhauer, K. (2014). *Forgotten connections. On culture and upbringing.* London: Routledge.

Richardson, V. (2003). Constructivist pedagogy. *Teachers College Record, 105,* 1623–1640.

Varela, F. J., Maturana, H. R., & Uribe, R. (1974). Autopoiesis: The organization of living systems, its characterization and a model. *Biosystems, 5,* 187–196.

Zhao, G. (2014). Freedom reconsidered: Heteronomy, open subjectivity, and the 'gift of teaching.' *Studies in Philosophy and Education, 33,* 513–525.

Zhao, G. (in press). From the philosophy of consciousness to the philosophy of difference: The subject of education after humanism. *Educational Philosophy and Theory.*

The Temporal Transcendence of the Teacher as Other

CLARENCE W. JOLDERSMA

Abstract

Over the last decades, education has shifted more clearly to a learner-centered understanding, including particularly constructivism, leaving little room conceptually for a substantive role for the teacher. This article develops a Levinasian framework for understanding the teacher as other. It begins by exploring the spatial metaphors of Levinas's idea of the teacher as transcendent but shifts to Levinas's idea of time as instants (durations) that come to the ego as a gift from the future. The article employs these temporal metaphors to understand better the transcendence of the teacher.

A recent critique of education's shift to a learning-centered paradigm insightfully observes that when the student as learner is moved to the center, teaching is conceptually reduced to a support role (Biesta, 2010, 2013). Even when learning from a teacher, the teacher is often reduced to a resource, depicted as facilitating learning by cueing the internal mechanisms of knowledge production. This model seems to have given up on the notion that students can learn something from the teacher. Constructivism is a good example of this paradigm (Fosnot, 2013), in which the learner is construed as constructing knowledge from within, as a kind of self-formation. Recently, it has been shown that constructivism is being co-opted by the neoliberal paradigm (Rodriguez, 2011). A construal of the teacher that resists its disappearance is now as important as ever.

One way to resist the disappearance of the teacher in education is to reimagine the relation between student and teacher. For this, I want to draw on Levinas's idea of the asymmetry between the self and the other. On this conception, the student's relation to the teacher is characterized asymmetrically. From the student's first-person perspective, the teacher is in the position of other (Biesta, 2006; Egéa-Kuehne, 2008; Joldersma, 2014; Todd, 2003). Depicting the relationship asymmetrically allows us to reestablish teaching as something independent of learning and, even more strongly, that which conditions the possibility of learning.

LEVINAS AND THE PHILOSOPHY OF EDUCATION

In this article, I will use the asymmetry of the student–teacher relation, but do so in the context of Levinas's more specific discussion of the teacher as transcendent. The teacher as transcendent makes possible learning something that one does not have the capability to possess currently. From the first-person perspective of the student, what comes from the other—the teacher—is something beyond one's own capacity as an ego. My aim was to provide a robust model to anchor substantive roles for teaching in education. I will first explore Levinas's spatial metaphors to describe the teacher as transcendent. Then, I will show their limitations and turn to Levinas's notion of time to develop a temporal understanding of the teacher's transcendence. This, I will argue, provides a robust way to portray the transcendence of the teacher.

The Spatial Metaphors Describing the Teacher as Transcendent

Both advocates and critics often use spatial metaphors to describe constructivism. For example, radical constructivist Ernst von Glasersfeld states that 'knowledge, no matter how it is defined, is *in the heads* of persons ...' (von Glasersfeld, 1995, p. 1; emphasis added). Similarly, Biesta's critique also uses spatial terms: 'constructivism sees the process of learning as *immanent*' (Biesta, 2013; emphasis added). For both advocate and critic of constructivism, learning is characterized as occurring *inside* the learner, *interior* to the subject's mind (Joldersma, 2011).

Similarly, Levinas's critique of consciousness and epistemology uses spatial metaphors. Levinas describes knowledge production using the metaphors of light and vision—our knowledge comes via vision, something that occurs in the light. Vision metaphors, in turn, show that knowledge acquisition remains immanent in the learner: 'The light that permits encountering something other than the self, makes it encountered as if it came from the ego' (Levinas, 1987, p. 68). The light metaphor shows that the ego's knowledge appears not to encounter anything that is truly exterior to itself, including objects in the outside world. More generally, for Levinas knowledge cannot establish a relationship with the world in its pure exteriority: 'It will not be knowledge, because through knowledge, whether one wants it or not, the object is absorbed by the subject and the duality disappears' (Levinas, 1987, p. 41). When the conscious subject has fulfilled its epistemological aim, the known object appears inside the horizon of the ego's consciousness as if produced by it. Levinas states, 'the object of consciousness, while distinct from consciousness, is as it were a product of consciousness, being a "meaning" endowed by consciousness ...' (Levinas, 1969, p. 123). Levinas's critique is couched in spatial metaphors: Knowledge production cannot be the avenue to pure exteriority, precisely because a central characteristic of knowledge is that it seems to be produced internally.

Levinas's use of spatial metaphors in his critique of knowledge production can help us criticize constructivism's learning-centeredness. Constructivism does not give a way of getting outside the head, remaining trapped in its interiority. Constructivism cannot model the student–teacher relation precisely because it cannot show how to get outside the ego. The core of its epistemological paradigm is a weakness for modeling intersubjectivity. When we wish to model the relation to the teacher as exterior in terms of *knowledge*, the alterity of the teacher gets interiorized by the learner's epistemological equipment. The grasp that constitutes comprehension is part of the ego's mastery over its own existence. Levinas says, 'the appearance of an existent is the very constitution of mastery over existing, of a freedom in existing ...' (Levinas, 1987, p. 52). The constructing subject, as a knowing ego, has no room for the teacher as other, because the ego functions with the freedom of synthesizing—turning what is sees into what is known. Constructivism, precisely because it is an epistemology, cannot model the relationship to the teacher as other. A student cannot be taught by the teacher on this model precisely because the learning process is characterized as immanent in the learner. Levinasian spatial metaphors form a strong critique of constructivism and learner-centeredness. They show why the teacher disappears from the scene in education.

Levinas's idea of the teacher as transcendent can help us resist such disappearance. The term 'teacher' for Levinas names the conditioning character of the other. Levinas says, 'the teacher who calls forth attention exceeds consciousness' (Levinas, 1969, p. 100). The teacher as other is outside of the consciousness of the student. This is not a mere overflowing of the student's consciousness, but 'a calling into question of the same' (p. 43)—it calls into question the student as an I, the spontaneity of the ego. Levinas is using the term 'teacher' not as 'a fact among others' (p. 70), namely, as an empirical person among others, but as the transcendent condition that makes such calling into question possible. Levinas states, 'It [teaching] is therefore to *receive* from the Other beyond the capacity of the I' (Levinas, 1969, p. 51). It is the relationship of the student to the teacher as transcendent that creates the conditions for the possibility of being taught by the teacher.

Levinas uses spatial metaphors to describe the transcendence of the teacher. He says, 'the teacher is *outside of* the consciousness he teaches' (Levinas, 1969, p. 100; emphasis added); 'It [being taught by] resides in the irreversibility of the relation between me and the other, in the Mastery of the Master coinciding with his position as other and as *exterior*' (p. 101; emphasis added). Levinas describes transcendence spatially, where the teacher as other is *outside* of the learner. In another passage, Levinas adds a new spatial metaphor: 'The calling in question of the I, coextensive with the manifestation of the Other in the face, we call language. The *height* from which language comes we designate with the term teaching' (Levinas, 1969, p. 171; emphasis added). Here, 'height' describes the transcendence of teaching—a spatial metaphor to depict how the teacher exceeds the I. If the student's consciousness is a container, then the metaphor of height describes the teacher in the position of *spatial* open-endedness—the uncontainability of the teacher's transcendence is signified by the metaphor of indefinitely extending spatially upward.

Eric Severson observes that in *Totality and Infinity*, Levinas is arguing against Heidegger's powerful ontology (Severson, 2013, p. 130). The experience of the infinite is meant to call into question that ontology is fundamental. Ontology is the relation with being. The exterior, as infinity, does not register and is incomprehensible in ontology. However, Severson argues, because of his disagreement with Heidegger, Levinas's own idea of transcendence remains entangled with the very ontological language he seeks to overcome, compromising the radicality of transcendence. This echoes Derrida's famous critique of Levinas. Derrida also is concerned that Levinas's language actually undermines his own project, including his ethical critique of Heidegger's ontology. Derrida argues that although Levinas is aware that the idea of exteriority is associated with totality and the ego, he nevertheless still develops the idea of the other 'by means of the Inside–Outside structure and by spatial metaphor' (Derrida, 1978, p. 112). Derrida's point is that Levinas does not complete his project consistently precisely because he uses spatial metaphors (Severson, 2013, p. 215). Derrida charges that Levinas's spatial metaphors continue to rely on spatially bound ideas which simultaneously are implicated in the ontological ideas that Levinas seeks to get beyond. Derrida's critique is, according to Severson, that 'if we can only designate radical alterity by way of negating finite spatial exteriority, then alterity can never be truly articulated outside of the scope of finitude' (2013, p. 217). This means that Levinas's depiction of alterity is bound not only to spatial exteriority, but also to the finitude of the immanence of presence. Severson suggests that this undermines Levinas's project of theorizing the other in a way that it remains transcendent, rather than being reabsorbed into the ego.

This concern applies also to Levinas's use of spatial metaphors to depict his idea of the teacher's transcendence. The spatial metaphors highlight the interiority of the student as subject and the exteriority of the teacher as transcendent. The metaphor of exteriority is meant to secure the idea of receiving something from beyond the student's own interiority, where the idea of exteriority marks non-possession and non-comprehension. Levinas expands the metaphor of exteriority with that of height to bring us an idea of uncontainability. This suggests that to be transcendent, non-overlapping interior–exterior fields are not enough. In 'height', the teacher's transcendence has to do with its lack of containment in a bounded area, an upward unboundedness that has no spatial border. But this means that the teacher's transcendence is described ultimately in terms of the negation of finite spatial exteriority. Using Severson's critique, this also means that this description cannot totally escape the scope of finitude that it is designed to overcome.

Although Levinas's spatial metaphors do give the transcendence of the teacher considerable strength, Severson and Derrida persuasively argue that they also compromise its radicality. Exteriority, as Derrida might say, remains caught up in the metaphysics of presence. Anything exterior is potentially interiorized—taken in hand, grasped, comprehended. As exterior, it exists in the same present and thus is always potentially given into the presence of the subject. The non-overlapping nature the interior–exterior fields is not enough of a barrier to resist this completely. Introducing infinity into exteriority helps, for it signals something out of reach of the ever present possibility of interiorization and comprehension. However, I agree with Severson and Derrida that spatial infinity is not radical enough. The teacher remains present even in the heights. My concern is that when we use only spatial metaphors to depict the teacher in the position of transcendence, the interiorizing reach of epistemology can always reenter the picture. As Levinas warns, the ego's vision can reach far into the exterior. And then, whatever is present is not radically out of reach of the learning self, the constructing ego—and we have constructivism back again. The idea of presence intrinsic in the spatial metaphors risks collapsing the student–teacher relation back into constructivism's learner-centered paradigm.

Reinterpreting Constructivism Temporally

There is another set of metaphors Levinas uses to describe the transcendence of the other, one that is more radical than his spatial metaphors. To develop them, I will return to Levinas's early books as well as his last major work. In these books, Levinas develops *temporal* metaphors for understanding transcendence, a mode I believe can fruitfully anchor his spatial metaphors describing the teacher as transcendent.

In *Existence and Existents*, Levinas develops his early idea of time through an innovative use of the notion of 'the instant'. Time has often been characterized as the successive passage of eternally present, infinitesimally small moments, something that can be measured by the beat of a clock. Time, on this understanding, is a series of punctual now's, where each successive moment replaces the previous one in a sweep of continuity. Levinas's critique of this idea, similar to Heidegger's, is that this view of time is a derivative understanding of something more primary, at least as an *experience* of time. Levinas uses Bergson's idea of duration (*durée*)—a non-punctual understanding of the idea of an instant—to develop an alternative. Severson points out that for Bergson the deep sense of time's motion cannot be measured, in part because it is always exposed to interruption: 'This sense of passage through time precedes the capacity for measure and is rendered abstract under the time-measuring tools of science' (2013, p. 52). Time for Bergson is the very mobility of the movement of something. Time is ecstatic, each duration giving birth to a future duration. Hence, there is a continuity in the movement of successive durations, albeit more complex than clock time. Levinas accepts Bergson's idea that the instant has duration. He also accepts Bergson's attempt to give a non-spatial depiction of time, pointing to Bergson's analogy with music: 'In listening to a melody we are also following its entire duration' (Levinas, 2001, p. 21)—an instant has duration. But for Bergson, there is also a continuum from one duration to the next because each instant in its radicalized individuality is capable of giving birth to the next instant. This also means that each instant involves evanescence, namely, in its giving birth to the new one it fades away. It loses its mastery of the present as it loses its presence to the next instant.

Levinas's idea of the instant differs from Bergson's notion of time in terms of the connection between durations. He does so by connecting the idea of the instant to the phenomena of effort and fatigue of the ego. The instant for Levinas becomes the temporal present initiated by the ego's action, where 'Effort is the very effecting of the instant' (Levinas, 2001, p. 23). To act is to constitute the present by taking charge of it. In that sense, the instant is intimately connected to the ego's emergence out of what Levinas calls bare existence (*il y a*). Precisely because of this emergence, the instant (duration) is also marked by fatigue, where 'the time-lag of fatigue creates the interval in which the event of the present can occur ...' (Levinas, 2001, p. 25). The instant is the duration of an event initiated by the ego's effort which has its demise in the ego's fatigue. Or, said differently, the instant is one way to construe the upwelling of the personal subject out of anonymous existence, with an inevitable evanescence that threatens the ego's continuing existence as a subject. Rather than the instant being understood only as the key to freedom and the subject's sovereignty, it also exposes the subject's captivity or enchainment to the present. In this, Levinas calls into question the ego's power to dislodge itself from this instant and propel itself forward into the next instant (Severson, 2013, p. 58).

Levinas develops the idea of the birth of each new instant differently than Bergson. Instants do not follow each other automatically. For Bergson, the ego has the ability to give birth in the present instant to the following instant, and so forth, indefinitely, giving it freedom of self-formation that endures. For Levinas, the ego cannot initiate the birth of a new duration because of the ego's evanescence is associated with fatigue. Therefore, the ego does not have the freedom and self-mastery over time. Precisely because each instant is an accomplishment—'Each instant is a beginning, a birth' (Levinas, 2001, p. 75)—it is equally true that 'The evanescence of an instant constitutes its very presence' (Levinas, 2001, p. 76). Essential to each instant is that it cannot endure. The ego does *not* have the ability to bring about the next instant, and it cannot establish a permanent continuity. Precisely because the ego cannot join the present instant to future ones, there is no freedom of self-mastery, only that of beginnings which inevitably fade away. This negates the possibility of the power of the ego over any one instant to endure into the next one. The ego is thus not free and sovereign. Levinas has taken away Bergson's traditional connotations of the ego's power of self-mastery through giving birth to successive instants.

Levinas's critique of Bergson' idea of the succession of durations provides a robust critique of learner-centered constructivism. Connecting Bergson's notion of duration to Husserl's temporal language, we can see that any instant consists of retentions (things remembered) and protentions (things anticipated)—the duration itself is temporal. As Severson puts it, 'The relationship of the ego to the past and the future is a matter of the ego's freedom; the past is what is seized and carried forward in retention, and the future is what is chosen in freedom through protention' (2013, p. 34). In constructivism, learning is an activity of the subject involving the freedom of self-formation and continuity, where the knowing subject is free to construct and possess its knowledge. More particularly, the learner's self-formation is bound up with the ego's selection of past memories and future anticipations in the present duration. The temporality within a duration is what Levinas calls economic time, when the selected past and the chosen future remain embedded in the present instant. It is in economic time that the protentions into the future are foreseeable and the retentions of the past are rememberable. The learner's freedom of self-formation, the core of constructivism, occurs in economic time.

This does not get the learner to the next instant. The event of learning in constructivism can be characterized as the upwelling of the subjectivity of the student as an ego. The learner-centered act of construction is an event in the interval of the instant, brought on by the ego's effort. However, using Levinas's analysis, the act of learning is concluded by fatigue. The very essence of the event of self-learning is marked by evanescence within the same duration—within economic time. The learning event therefore does not signal the endurance of ego in the movement from one instant to the next, but is characterized by the ego's fatigue. This marks its fading away, an aging and death of the duration without renewal. In constructivism, the learner's ego remains enchained to the present instant. Because the learning event ends when fatigue sets in, the learning associated with constructivism is precisely not the freedom of self-mastery and self-constitution. The event of self-learning does not constitute the ego's ecstatic projection into *future* instants, but remains in the foreseeable present, within economic time. The learning event that constitutes the learner's ego weighs it down by its continuing enchainment to the present. The reason that constructivism as a theory is not adequate is that its view of time is internal to the instant—it remains bound to economic time. Constructivism cannot adequately characterize how the ego can get out of its own present instant. For that, the learner requires being taught by a teacher as transcendent, to get beyond what he or she can contain. Levinas's understanding of time can help us understand the problems with constructivism better.

Temporalizing the Transcendent

Levinas's insight with respect to time is that one instant does not give birth to the next through the action of the ego. Levinas empties the duration of the possibility of generating continuity with the next instant. Within each duration, there is temporality, but these are depicted as the ego's present memories (retentions) and anticipations (protentions), part of the ego's perceived ecstatic freedom within *economic* time. The radical future, found in the next instant, is not the foreseeable future. Although it is justifiable to argue for self-constitution as the ego moves through economic time, Levinas's point is that this remains enmeshed in the present instant and is never able to move itself into the next instant. The ego is never able to give birth to a genuinely unforeseeable future. In Levinasian terms, the optimism of constructivism's epistemological freedom is misplaced, for the learner's ego continues to be enchained in the present, merely fulfilling the potential of the student's present instant, in economic time. To learn something new, as if moving into the next duration, requires learning from a teacher, as other.

This requires the conditioning transcendence of the teacher to be temporal. Levinas says, 'If the present endured, it would have received its existence from something preceding' (Levinas, 1987, p. 53). Levinas radicalizes his understanding of time to solve this problem. He says, 'To shatter the enchainment of matter is to shatter the finality of hypostasis. It is to be in time' (Levinas, 1987, p. 57). Something Levinas calls 'time' is required to overcome the ego's enchainment in the instant, its evanescence. The ego needs something more than the temporality of economic time, that is, more than marking the flow *within* the present duration; it needs a temporality from one duration to the next. Perhaps unsurprisingly, Levinas connects this more radical notion of time to intersubjectivity. He states, 'time is not the achievement of an isolated and lone subject, but ... it is the very relationship of the subject with the Other' (Levinas, 1987, p. 39). The radicality of his idea is that time, the temporality connecting one duration to the next, is not to be found within the egoism of the epistemic subject, the isolated individual. Rather, 'time' names the relationship with the other.

Time becomes the solution to the problem of the ego's enchainment in the instant. The ego is powerless to give birth to the next instant, imprisoned in the present instant; time offers the possibility of moving to the next instant. Time indicates an event that happens to the ego which is not part of its current enchaining instant.

Levinas uses the temporal term 'the future' to articulate this movement: 'the future is what is not grasped, but what befalls us and lays hold of us' (Levinas, 1987, p. 77). The ego cannot actively grasp the next instant; rather, the ego is passive with respect to its coming. Time as the future is the time of new birth arising not as an extension of the present instant, but as something radically foreign, coming in from the future. For that, it must be something that befalls the ego. The subject is passive in the coming of the next instant.

More concretely, the future shows up in the other. Levinas says, 'The other is the future. The very relationship with the other is the relationship with the future' (Levinas, 1987, p. 77). The asymmetric relation to the other is a relation to the future. The other *is* the future, in the present, for the passive ego. The future is the coming of the other, as something completely other. This is someone who has not yet arrived, namely, not yet absorbed into the ego's present instant. The relationship with the other is a relationship with the future, a temporally inflected absence that cannot be made present in the present instant.

The future's coming arrives as a *gift* to the subject (Severson, 2013, p. 60). Despite the economic time within the duration, Levinas construes the present instant as a kind of a temporal prison for the subject. The enchainment of the subject in the instant means that its redemption by the future cannot arise from within the present. Time is an unforseeable gift that redeems the subject. As an unforeseen gift, the other as the future makes possible the transition between successive instants for the ego. The transition involves forgiveness: The present instant receives a pardon from the other, releasing the ego from the eternal present. From within the instant, from the perspective of the ego, the other as the future is a gift, experienced as radical hope. In Levinas's words, 'what produces the thrust of hope is the gravity of the instant in which it occurs. The irreparable is its natural atmosphere. There is hope only when hope is no longer permissible' (2001, p. 91). The instant's impotence to bring in the future is an irreparability, rightly leaving the ego without hope. Radical hope is the ego's felt desire to transcend the present instant with something not anticipatable and yet not settling for the irreparable present. Although without the muscular power of ego-initiated change, radical hope liberates the ego from the economic time of the present by transforming the finality of the present into something unfinished. Hope undoes the ego's experienced enchainment to the present, making incomplete what seemed complete and determined, creating an expectation for a future that goes beyond the reasonable anticipations of the present circumstances. As such, radical hope undermines the completeness and supposed novelty of constructivism's claims that the self-learning subject is the complete story. The instant is given new life, as it were, through hope brought by the other as the future rather than by means of self-constructed knowledge. The redemption of the instant comes through the other as temporally transcendent.

Redemption of the instant is something that breaks through the present in the ego's relation to the other. Levinas says, 'time is constituted by my relation to the other, it is exterior to my instant, but it is also something else than an object given to contemplation' (Levinas, 2001, p. 96). Time is a gift that comes from the other as the future. Although he reverts to a spatial metaphor, 'exterior to my instant,' the other is not synchronous with that present, but is experienced as the unexpected future. Precisely because it is the future, the other remains transcendent, outside the ego's rational understanding and self-constituting knowledge. The other as future gives time to the ego, as a gift. And in giving time, the other gives the subject freedom, precisely not as self-mastery, but in the ego's present duration being pardoned, something that comes from the other. Hope brings the expectation of the possibility of movement beyond the present duration, to fix what appears unfixable, to undo the fatigue that is a time-delayed end of the present instant. The ego's freedom is in the hands of the other as the future.

Time is an intersubjective relation bridging a temporal gap between the present instant and the incoming future, one that cannot be spanned by the ego. Concretely, the relation to the future is the intersubjective relation to the other, permanently located beyond the synchrony needed for the ego's assimilation, because the other is in a time that is not in the ego's present. It is the temporal character of the gap that resists absorption by the ego. The other's resistance is its future location, beyond the reaches of the ego, who is constrained to working in the present. Beyond economic time, the ego's more primordial sense of time is experienced in the relation with the other, as incoming futurity. The future is always ahead of the ego's power of mastery and control. This means that the future is not a mere extension and fulfillment of the ego's present potentials and possibilities, but arrives through their incalculable, unpredictable, unforeseeable disturbances. The other as the future is what moves the ego past its present possibilities. In its rescue of the self's enchainment, time is a gift from the other.

In his last major work, Levinas calls this temporal relation *diachrony* (Levinas, 1998, pp. 9–10). Levinas uses diachrony to name the radical passivity of ego, something lurking below all the activity of the ego in its present instant. The encounter with the other takes the form of diachrony, an idea that circumvents the synchrony of his previous spatial metaphors, as well as the synchrony of economic time (Severson, 2013, p. 190). The evidence of the encounter is an irreducible disturbance by something futural that is not present in the present. The time that constitutes diachrony protects the other from being assimilated back into the synchrony of economic time, because the disturbance itself signifies a trace from the future that is unrepresentable and unassimilable in the present. The trace of the other is felt diachronically, because it interrupts the ego's anticipations within the duration.

Temporalizing the Teacher as Transcendent

It is now time to return more directly to Levinas's idea of the teacher as transcendent. Although cast in temporal terms, from the perspective of the student, the teacher is still in the position of the other; further, being taught by a teacher is still something that comes from beyond the self of the student. It still befalls the student. But when we use Levinas's temporal metaphors to depict the transcendence of teaching, then what befalls the student comes from a time that is not in the student's present duration. It comes from a radical future. It is the teacher as the future that lays hold of the student as a learning ego. A temporal metaphor depicts the idea of 'learning more that contains the I.' The transcendence of the teacher cannot be contained in the learning ego's present, and thus not in the ego's presence. The teacher as transcendent, felt as something radically foreign, comes in as a disrupting future, unsettling the ego by coming into the present instant from a different time. The teacher as the future disturbs the economic time of the student, the learner in the present duration. The student receives something from beyond his or her capacity as a self-learner in the present.

The economic time of retentions and protentions that constitute present learning experiences is transcended by something from the future. The disturbances of the learner's economic time are not hostile or violent, but are welcomed by the learning ego. This warmly received disturbance enters the present as something unexpected, an unpredicted gift. It comes as a welcome surprise, something the ego in the present instant could not have known. The surprise of getting to the next instant is a release from the present, a kind of slippage from the enchainment. The unexpected gift that constitutes getting beyond the present instant is a pardon, a forgiveness of the present instant. The disturbance by the teacher as temporally transcendent effects a pardon of the learning effort of the student, creating a slippage which allows the learning ego to escape the present instant. As a pardon, the surprising gift that constitutes being taught by a teacher makes possible the student's slippage from the present, allowing the possibility of the birth of something radically new, a new instant. In short, the teacher as a transcendent future constitutes the gift of transcending the present instant for the learning ego.

The learning ego's welcome of the teacher as temporally transcendent shows up in the present as the ego's radical hope. This is the student's desire to transcend the present instant with something the ego cannot anticipate. This is not the ego's anticipatory constructions, which would keep the student enchained in the present instant. Without the felt desire of radical hope, the ego will settle for the irreparable present of the instant's economic time. The radical hope of the learning ego, a response to the gift of pardon from the teacher as the future, undoes the experienced enchainment to the present instant, making incomplete what seems complete and determined. The felt hope creates an openness and expectation for a future that goes beyond any reasonable expectation of the present instant. The time of being taught by a teacher as transcendent is experienced as radical hope for something genuinely new coming in from the future.

The gift of being taught by a teacher as transcendent is temporal. As a temporal gift, it comes from the teacher as if from the future. Because the teacher as other is situated in the future for the student, the transcendence of the teacher is radical. What separates the learning ego from the teacher is a diachronic gap that cannot be bridged by the student, for the time of the teacher is not synchronous with the learning ego's present instant. The time of being taught by a teacher is an intersubjective relation constituted as a temporal gap felt by the student as an unexpected future. The otherness of the teacher is a function of a futurity that cannot be recovered into the learning ego's present instant. The student's primordial experience of the time of being taught is experienced in the relation to the teacher as transcendent, as an incoming futurity that surprises.

LEVINAS AND THE PHILOSOPHY OF EDUCATION

The time of being taught by the teacher as other redeems the present. Redemption through the teacher as the future comes precisely because the learning ego is locked into the present instant, which it cannot escape. This redemption involves diachrony. It is diachronic because the ego's present instant is opened up by the future to something better that the learning subject cannot anticipate. Diachronic time breaks into the student's present instant, coming in from the future by disturbing the learner's inner economy, redeeming it by opening it up to what the student cannot contain. Redemption releases the student from its enchainment to the present instant. The breakthrough of diachronic time in being taught by a teacher as transcendent is experienced as a gift allowing the student to have a genuine relation to the future he cannot anticipate. In the student's relation to the teacher as other, she experiences the redemption—release from the captivity of the present instant. The diachrony of being taught by a teacher is a temporal disturbance that releases the student from the bonds of the present, allowing genuine learning to occur. This gives a substantive role for the teacher in the educational event.

Disclosure statement

No potential conflict of interest was reported by the author.

References

Biesta, G. J. J. (2006). *Beyond learning: Democratic education for a human future*. Boulder, CO: Paradigm.

Biesta, G. J. J. (2010). *Good education in an age of measurement: Ethics, politics, democracy*. Boulder, CO: Paradigm.

Biesta, G. J. J. (2013). Receiving the gift of teaching: From "learning from" to "being taught by". *Studies in Philosophy and Education, 32*, 449–461. doi:10.1007/s11217-012-9312-9

Derrida, J. (1978). Violence and metaphysics: An essay on the thought of Emmanuel Levinas. In A. Bass (Trans.), *Writing and difference* (pp. 97–192). Chicago, IL: University of Chicago Press.

Egéa-Kuehne, D. (Ed.). (2008). *Levinas and education: At the intersection of faith and reason*. London: Routledge.

Fosnot, C. T. (2013). *Constructivism: Theory, perspectives, and practice* (2nd ed.). New York, NY: Teachers College Press.

Joldersma, C. W. (2011). Ernst von Glasersfeld's radical constructivism and truth as disclosure. *Educational Theory, 61*, 275–293. doi:10.1111/j.1741-5446.2011.00404.x

Joldersma, C. W. (2014). *A levinasian ethics for education's commonplaces*. London: Palgrave Pivot.

Levinas, E. (1969). *Totality and infinity: An essay on exteriority.* (A. Lingis, Trans.). Pittsburgh, PA: Duquesne University Press.

Levinas, E. (1987). *Time and the other.* (R. A. Cohen, Trans.). Pittsburgh, PA: Duquesne University Press.

Levinas, E. (1998). *Otherwise than being: Or beyond essence.* (A. Lingis, Trans.). Pittsburgh, PA: Duquesne University Press.

Levinas, E. (2001). *Existence and existents.* (A. Lingis, Trans.). Pittsburgh, PA: Duquesne University Press.

Rodriguez, E. (2011). Constructivism and the neoliberal agenda in the Spanish curriculum reform of the 1980s and 1990s. *Educational Philosophy and Theory, 43,* 1047–1064. doi:10.1111/j.1469-5812.2009.00613.x

Severson, E. (2013). *Levinas's philosophy of time: Gift, responsibility, diachrony, hope.* Pittsburgh, PA: Duquesne University Press.

Todd, S. (2003). *Learning from the other: Levinas, psychoanalysis, and ethical possibilities in education.* Albany, NY: SUNY Press.

von Glasersfeld, E. (1995). *Radical constructivism.* London: Routledge Falmer.

Education Incarnate

SHARON TODD

Abstract

For the past 15 years, scholars in education have focused on Levinas's work largely in terms of his understanding of alterity, of the self-Other relation, of ethics as 'first philosophy' and the significance these concepts have on rethinking educational theory and practice. What I do in this paper, by way of method, is to start from a slightly different place, from the assertion that there is indeed something 'new' to be explored in Levinas's philosophy – both in terms of ideas to be found within his work, and also in terms of the demands educational ideas and practices place on his work from without. That is, how does the actual, lived specificity of educational encounters occasion a different set of questions than one would otherwise pose if thinking only from within the discipline of philosophy, or from a purely theoretical point of view? In light of this, this paper explores Levinas's ideas of sensibility, materiality, and embodiment. I see these not simply as supports for his ethical thought, but as the very core of incarnation without which his ethics makes no sense. I propose that these ideas are quintessentially pedagogical aspects of his thought – that is, they are always already rooted in a relational context of change and alteration of the subject.

Sensation is the break-up of every system.

Levinas, *Totality and Infinity*, p. 63

For the past 15 years, scholars in education have focused on Levinas's work largely in terms of his understanding of alterity, of the self–Other relation, of ethics as 'first philosophy' and the significance these concepts have on rethinking educational theory and practice (Biesta, 2006; Chinnery, 2003; Egéa-Kuehne, 2008; Todd, 2003, 2008). Although some have focused explicitly on teacher–student relations (Joldersma, 2002; Säfström, 2003), others put his work into relation with curriculum (Standish, 2008; Winter, 2014) and counter the educational aim of autonomy with his notion of heteronomy (Kodelja, 2008; Strhan, 2009). Given the extent to which Levinas's philosophy is no longer a stranger to educational audiences, it is difficult to see, perhaps, what more could be said, said differently, or said with different purposes in mind without rehashing some well-known territory. This is particularly the case if we, as both Levinas scholars and educationalists, continue to think of his primary—or sole—contribution to education as resting in what has in fact already been said. Indeed, what more is there to say about or do with his work?

In a recent collection, entitled *Radicalising Levinas* (2010), the editors discuss precisely this question. They identify Levinasian scholarship in terms of three waves: the first being commentary and exposition from the 1970s and 1980s; the second one concerned with contextualising Levinas's work in poststructuralism and deconstruction; and the current, third wave can be seen as a revitalisation of his scholarship in placing his ideas in relation to 'the most pressing socio-political issues of our time' (p. x). Levinas's work, in this third wave, offers itself to the forging of new connections with, for example, world hunger (Bernasconi, 2010); animals (Atterton, 2012; Calarco, 2010; Perpich, 2008); climate change (Edelglass, 2012; Simmons, 2012); and ecology (Llewelyn, 2010). In line with this, the educational reception of Levinas's philosophy in the past primarily falls within the first and second waves. The third wave would now seem to be on the horizon. However, what all three 'waves' assume, I contend, is that 'Levinas's philosophy' itself is a relatively stable entity and that it is mainly in conversation with contemporary problems that it can begin to take on new significance. While I think that his work does indeed speak to contemporary educational concerns, I nonetheless want to suggest that there are elements of his work that have remained somewhat overshadowed by the weightier concepts of the Face and the Other, for which he is best known.

What I do in this article, by way of method, is to start from a slightly different place, from the assertion that there is indeed something 'new' to be explored in Levinas's philosophy—both in terms of ideas to be found *within* his work, and also in terms of the demands educational ideas and practices place on his work from *without*. From the perspective of exploring something new within his philosophy, I do not mean to suggest that we can 'find' or 'excavate' a concept that no one has before seen; as though there were some secret treasure buried in the Levinasian archives just waiting to be dug out, which, once discovered, will turn our traditional frameworks of interpretation on their head. Instead, it consists in a far more modest gesture of displacing and repositioning his thought in such a way that new life is breathed into it. Concepts, such as the Face or the Other, can thereby take on new nuances once they are untethered from tightly constrained systems of meaning. Thus, newness, as I see it here, is not about 'discovering' or 'uncovering' a hidden truth, but about allowing ideas to circulate in a novel relationship to other ideas that might not have been previously high up on the Levinasian agenda. This displacement and repositioning shifts the grounds upon which an idea or concept has come to be comprehended and thereby shifts our own relationship to it. Although such newness can arise from philosophical reflection on Levinas's work, it is not through philosophy alone that such newness comes about. Rather, I suggest that newness arises out of the very demands that the lived conditions of education place on his ideas and concepts. By this I mean that rather than see educational contexts as sites of application for Levinas's philosophy, newness emerges in reading his ideas through the specificity of teaching and learning encounters. That is, how does the actual, lived specificity of those encounters occasion a different set of questions than one would otherwise pose if thinking only from within the discipline of philosophy, or from a purely theoretical point of view? For me, such specificity—the design of the classroom, the mode of instruction, the vulnerability of teachers, the fear of students, the absorption in a topic, the specific smells and sounds and touches of other bodies—places a certain demand on Levinas's ethical philosophy that, I argue, is not entirely out of joint with the very trajectory of his thought.

In light of this, this article explores that which, in my view, is not focused on enough in both the philosophical and educational literatures on Levinas—that is, his ideas of sensibility, materiality and embodiment. I see these not simply as supports for his ethical thought, but as the very core of incarnation without which his ethics makes no sense. Tom Sparrow's (2013) recent examination of the materialist and metaphysical as well as the phenomenological aspects of Levinas's ethics will be my point of departure for displacing and resituating key ideas within the educational reception of Levinas, namely, the Face and the Other. Through this, I propose that his views of sensibility and embodiment are quintessentially pedagogical aspects of his thought—that is, they are always already rooted in a relational context of change and alteration of the subject—a process through which one becomes someone 'beyond' the limits of one's previous incarnation.[1] In conclusion, I turn to a discussion of how embodiment and sensibility are ethical features of educational life, insofar as educational settings are indeed concerned with the pedagogical transformation of the self. However, before doing so, I turn now to situate the question of embodiment within an educational context.

Situating the Pedagogical Question of Embodiment

Questions of embodiment and materiality have recently been the theme of much contemporary discussion in educational practice, research methodology and theorising (e.g. Davies, 2009; Lenz Taguchi, 2011; Special Issue of Gender and Education, 2013). This body of literature has largely, although not exclusively, grown out of a feminist and Deleuzian orientation to education, seeing the active transformation of subjectivity in terms that radically admit of the agentic aspects of materiality. Human bodies are put on par with the objects with which they interact.[2] That is, embodiment and materiality are not so much woven together as they are mutually constitutive, each change calling forth new possibilities for subjectivity. There is here an emphasis on activity and movement, materiality itself being seen not in terms of substance, but as a constellation of processes. Human bodies are therefore not seen to be merely the physical counterpart to a self, but part of the very materiality that comprises any space. This literature opens up important questions for education regarding its production of spaces of materiality as necessary conditions for teaching, and indeed, for the kinds of subject transformation that projects such as feminism are particularly eager to engage. However, what is not so much in focus in this rendering of educational space, are the *sensible* aspects of human materiality as this materiality in the form of human bodies is generated through the unpredictable contact with the non-human materiality within its environment. That is, in these moments of contact between things, how do the sensations produced in classrooms —the touch of the keyboard, the sweatiness of a hand I am holding, the smell of perfume, the grooves of the desk—matter to the constitution of the body, its surfaces and borders?

Elspeth Probyn (2004), in an article discussing the place of affect and bodies in teaching, suggests that the body in particular has been elided (perhaps surprisingly so) within critical and feminist pedagogies. Her claim is largely based on what she sees as an abstraction of the 'live body' into complex theory.[3] That is, while there is a plethora of theories about how the body is constituted through power dynamics, normative discourses and systems of discrimination, little attention is paid to the role played by singular affect. For Probyn, there seems to be a 'retreat from the experiential body' (p. 23) in these pedagogies. Instead, drawing in part, although not exclusively, on Deleuze, she notes the significance of affect and sensibility in the concrete constitution of the form of materiality known as the human body. She sees Deleuze's notion of ethology as particularly inviting. He describes it thus: 'a body affects other bodies, or is affected by other bodies; it is this capacity for affecting and being affected that also defines a body in its individuality' (Deleuze quoted in Probyn, 2004, p. 37). As such, 'ethology studies the compositions of relations or capacities between different things' (ibid).

As one such relation, a relation that encapsulates the experiential dimensions of the body, Probyn seeks to bring to the attention of her students what she calls '"the goose bump effect"—that moment when a text sets off a frisson of feelings, remembrances, thoughts, and the bodily actions that accompany them' (p. 29). In fact, by inviting students to explore an effect of reading that is 'wild, diffuse and hard to properly name' (ibid), Probyn also invites the body into direct contact with what is going on in classrooms, without, however, suggesting that experiential and sensible aspects of bodies are unrelated to previous circumstances. 'What constitutes an affective response is hugely complex, and is in part the result of an embodied history to which and with which the body reacts, including how the classroom is conceived and practiced' (p. 29). For Probyn, education is about facing the 'live subject', complete with discomforts, embarrassments and excitements that close contact with other bodies, and with texts, generate. Unlike previous 'transgressive' theories of the body that have played a role in feminist discussions of pedagogy, such as that developed by Jane Gallop (1995, 1997), Probyn seeks to move beyond the body as being 'engulfed in the sexual' (p. 34). This strikes me as a highly significant move, not in order to deny the desirous and sometimes rapturous effects of bodies in classroom situations, but to open up the terrain for investigating a plethora of sensibilities and affects that constitute the lived experience of classroom education.

What Probyn's work brings to the fore is a combination of the new materialism, which sees bodies as 'modes not substances', and a rigorous attention to the unpredictable arrangement of affect and sensibility that is involved in constituting these modes.

How better to explain that always quirky, always unknowable combination that is the classroom? Why is it, we ask either in elation or depression, that the same material will work so differently in different situations? The magic or chemistry that seems so elusive to any systemization may well be the necessary result of the moving arrangement of particles, histories and affects that are the bodies of teaching and learning. (p. 37)

If changes in bodies are occasioned by these unpredictable and unknowable relations between things, then the transformative potential of feminist or critical pedagogies is equally uncertain, and no longer tied to the effects of a particular discourse, theory or practice. Rather, the pedagogical transformation of the subject is more in line with what Luce Irigaray would call the 'alchemy' of subjectivity and less dependent upon what critical and feminist pedagogues would call consciousness-raising. Introducing this unpredictably, however, into our educational discussions should not be seen as some nihilist defeat of pedagogical purpose, but instead as the generative potential for moving beyond the systemisation and organisation of teaching and learning into discrete elements. That is, this rather anarchic sensibility challenges the assumption that the 'right' kind of teaching will produce the 'right' learning outcomes. As such, it offers a powerful critique against the types of managerialism and performativity-based frameworks for systemising teaching and learning we are finding on a global scale. As Levinas (1969) himself acknowledges in the epigraph to this article, 'sensibility is the break-up of every system'; sensibility is precisely that which cannot be contained, directed or enforced by tightly defined procedures and institutional arrangements. Probyn's call for exposing the centrality of the 'live subject' for classroom contexts, thereby opens up a way of thinking pedagogical transformation that necessarily takes into account the way bodies also transcend (and are not merely products of) structure and system. Moreover, paying serious attention to the 'live subject' means acknowledging the sensible body, without which words such as 'encounters', 'teaching' and 'learning' make little sense. What Probyn in effect exposes (although this is not her primary purpose) is that you cannot have an educational *practice*—or any practice for that matter—without 'live subjects' in the first place.

It might seem as though we have come a long way from the Levinasian understanding of self and Other that has heretofore dominated discussions within education. However, as I explore below, there is a profound attunement to sensibility and the experiential, embodied subject in Levinas's thought that complements Probyn's call for exposing the corporeal dimensions of the classroom. What Levinas's work brings to the table that is not suggested by the new materialism is how bodily sensibility opens up deeper questions of transcendence and the transformation of bodies that this entails. My task for the rest of the article is to discuss how such embodied transcendence is central to the pedagogical project of transformation.

Embodiment, Materiality and Transcendence

I often get a sense when reading Levinas's depiction of subjectivity, especially in *Otherwise than Being*, of a subject who is cast into a winter desert, cold and unprotected from the winds, alone with others and burdened with the inevitability of the death of oneself and all beings. The subject is at once vulnerable and sacrificial, wounded and bound, defenceless and subordinate. Out of all this, the subject rises to respond (responsibly) to the command of the Other, in a relation of physical proximity, of nearness, of facing. Images of almost unbearable poignancy are brought to mind: the subject is naked, skinless, helpless and exposed. They are strikingly bleak images. And while they are no strangers to the landscape of existentialism, haunted as that landscape is with the approaching horizon of death towards which the subject is borne without choice or consent, they do seem rather ill-suited to the scene of a classroom.

However, these images of the subject invoked by Levinas are also striking, I think, because they call forth a radical sense of embodiment. That is, these images are not merely metaphors for a subject whose naked skin is vulnerable to the elements and the passing of human time. Rather, such images of embodiment call forth a 'reality' insofar as they seek to approach through language, the pulsing sensibilities that arise in experiencing the vicissitudes of life. As Bergo (2014) puts it: 'The central wager of *Otherwise than Being* is to express affectivity in its immediacy, with minimal conceptualisation'. Yet, these images also call forth a 'transcendence' insofar as it is through an inarticulable embodied relation to the Other that one's ego surpasses its limitations. On the surface of things, this way of casting embodiment, in terms of both sensibility and transcendence, would seem to be contradictory, and perhaps somewhat removed from the notion of the body I discussed above in relation to education. However, as Sparrow (2013) points out, it is at the intersection of embodiment, materiality and metaphysics where Levinas's work gets really interesting. Indeed, here we find how sensibility and transcendence strangely meet. My intention here is to explore Levinasian embodiment in order to get a sense of how his work actually helps to extend and illuminate the question of the sensible body as an eminently pedagogical one.

Sparrow, with a fresh and irreverent tone, begins his adventure into Levinas's philosophy by exposing him as 'someone explicitly engaged in the establishment of a materialist account of subjectivity' (p. 3), and one that is committed to 'thinking the insubstantiality of the subject' (p. 55). His oblique way of reading Levinas as a philosopher of materiality opens up the question as to how, if embodiment is indeed paramount, we assume the emergence of subjectivity through our contact with others who are radically different from our selves. To do this, Levinas takes recourse through sensation. As a philosopher heavily influenced by phenomenology, the experiential dimensions of subjectivity remain at the heart of the self–Other relation. However, what Sparrow (2013) notes is that 'logic of sensation identified by Levinas is not something disclosed phenomenologically. It is, as Deleuze says, invisible' (p. 23). As Levinas (1987) himself explains:

> It is a relationship with the In-visible, where invisibility results not from some incapacity of human knowledge, but from the inaptitude of knowledge as such—from its in-adequation—to the Infinity of the absolutely other, and from the absurdity that an event such as coincidence would have here. (p. 32)

That is, when Levinas discusses the encounter with the Other, he does not suggest that the Other 'appears' to me, and then can be read and understood through my sensations and perceptions. Quite the opposite. It is the mystery and unknowability of the Other that 'reveal' themselves. This 'invisibility' is precisely what is suggested when Levinas claims that when we truly face the Other, we do not even notice the colour of her eyes.[4] That is, as a gestalt, the embodied Other remains independent of the intentionality of the self, or the grasping of the self, as one who seeks to know the Other through concepts, categories and distinctions. Sparrow (2013) suggests, I think rightly, that 'the body lives a time that is out of step with the ego. It signals a reality that belongs to the sensible dimension of any spectacle, and which Levinas can only describe as a kind of magical evasion of presence' (p. 27). What happens through sensation is that we are 'directly' brought into the relation; it occasions 'a submersion of oneself' in the 'vitality of sensation' (p. 33). Indeed, Levinas (1998) claims that it is not our knowledge of sensation, but the act of sensing that matters to his ethics.

> The sensible qualities—sounds, colors, hardness, softness—are attributes of things; but they also seem to be lived in time in the form of psychic life, stretching out or dividing in the succession of temporal phases, and not only lasting or being altered in the measurable time of physicists. (p. 31)

What is important to keep in mind here is that such directness lies outside the field of concepts and categories. Sensation is not a 'phenomenon' or an 'appearance', but a rhythm or vibration experienced directly through contact. Sparrow (2013) writes, 'Sensation does not need to be communicated through a sign, symbol, or concept. It is the body that comprehends, or rather accommodates, the power of sensation' (p. 33).

Now, this raises some interesting questions for education, and for understanding embodied forms of affect more generally. As Ahmed (2004) has written, affect circulates as a form of social currency, and perhaps cannot simply be read so 'directly' as Sparrow is implying. For example, how might cultural practices function to sculpt a particularly bodily response to a given set of stimuli? How might a Muslim student experience bodily sensations of fear or pride or resolve in learning that she is not allowed to wear her hijab in her non-Muslim school? Are such bodily reactions not always already culturally or socially coded? My response is that following Levinas, and his move to transcendence, the *kind* of sensation one experiences may indeed be read, named and interpreted, but that the experience of sensation itself lies in a state prior to language. That is, embodied responses, such as Probyn's 'goose-bump effect', are not first about meaning or content (e.g. goose-bumps can *mean* many things: fear, pleasure, eroticism and anxiety), but are first corporeal processes upon which we lay over our concepts and categories, after the fact as it were. What this suggests is how to think of the transformative aspects of education as embodying untheorised experience as opposed to already assuming we know what students 'feel' when they 'sense' goose-bumps. This is definitely not to suggest that affects cannot or should not be analysed, but that there also needs to be some room made for untheorised experience in our classrooms if we are going, paradoxically, to 'understand' the specifically ethical dimensions of teaching and the transformation implied therein. I return to this idea more fully in the conclusion. Suffice for now to say that what is at stake in viewing embodied sensibility as a direct effect of contact with others (human and non-human alike) is that it opens the subject up to a plurality of possibilities that are based on not knowing, on something prior to naming experience.

The unknowability of the Other is not merely a trope for suggesting that the other is an object that appears to me beyond my current frames of cognition, and with other, better lenses I can come to 'know' her better; it is, rather, that the Other is that which disturbs my sense of knowing, my ego and my identity. And this is where the phenomenological approach to sensibility hits its limits. That is, Levinas cannot fully follow through on the idea that the Other, who occasions sensation, is only something (or someone) who 'appears' to me. Instead, there is something of the Other hidden from view because she 'is' more than an appearance. This logic suggests that my sensations of the Other can never fully capture her limits, since those limits exceed my very perception. 'Sensation allows his [Levinas's] other to "escape closure", precisely because sensation is what allows us to make contact with exteriority without subjecting that exteriority to our representational devices' (Sparrow, 2013, p. 109). To embrace phenomenology too closely would mean that the sensations invoked in relation to the Other remain confined within the ego's purview and this risks becoming a self-sustaining system, where the other becomes reduced to what *I* can know and perceive. But since the Other breaks up the totality of my identity (Levinas, 1969), breaks up systems (Levinas, 1969, p. 63) and breaks up essence (Levinas, 1998, p. 14), it needs to exist as a body in its own right, and not merely present itself as an object of my perception. As Perpich (2008) writes in countering the phenomenological critique against Levinas:

> the problem of transcendence that is the spur to Levinas's philosophy is precisely the problem of whether these [phenomenological] categories and modes of evaluation exhaust the whole of what is, or whether there is not in human experience a moment of transcendence when the sway of our relation to the world is pierced by another order, a sociality in which the other 'appears' not only as a thing among things or a force ranged against us but as a singular being who 'counts as such' and whose meaning, therefore, is not a function of a larger system or whole but signifies outside of every horizon or context. (pp. 48–49)

However, another problem of transcendence is the kind of generalisation it introduces into the field of sensibility. That is, if sensation and affect are central to the ethical relation between I and the Other, which Levinas claims it is, then how can sensation ever be about the 'absolute unknowability' and 'enigma' of the Other? Would this not entail a shift away from the Other's concrete face, her smell, her voice, her touch? Sparrow (2013) expresses his worry thus:

> But it could be argued that enigmas are practically unsatisfactory and leave too much to presumption, a loyal ally of discrimination. To allow the Other to remain enigmatic and absolutely beyond recognition—as Levinas must, since this is what makes his philosophy innovative—is to claim that the

imperative the Other commands issues from elsewhere, from some unmarked locale. That is, some place where my body cannot be and therefore cannot hear. How do I even begin to respond appropriately to such a call? When the alterity of the Other is deemed absolute, we overlook the fact that racism often thrives on such a disregard for the phenomenality of the face ... It seems to me that Levinas ought to have made the color of the Other's eyes—along with the rest of his/her phenomenal features—an essential feature of the Other's singularity. Even if he doesn't completely dismiss such features, Levinas does not attribute enough significance to the phenomenal in his account of faciality. (p. 93)

While one can wish that Levinas articulated things differently, I do think that his decision to move beyond the phenomenal positions bodily sensation on a different register. That is, although sensations occur in the 'immediacy of the sensible' (1998, p. 62), they also are tied to a response to the Other that cannot, for Levinas, be 'determined' by thought or categories of the sensible. Instead, it is both affecting and being affected by that constitute the responsible subject. This means that there is both vulnerability and suffering on the one hand, and nourishment, enjoyment and giving, on the other. 'This immediacy [of the sensible] is first of all the ease of enjoyment, more immediate than drinking, the sinking into the depths of the element, into its incomparable freshness, a plenitude and a fulfilment' (Levinas, 1998, p. 64). As Sparrow (2013) himself notes:

> Although in the final analysis vulnerability is the defining feature of sensibility for Levinas, it is also a site of what he calls *alimentation*. Sensations are not only what threaten to break up identities, they are also what nourish identities. Our bodies metabolize sensations and thereby incorporate them into their constitution. Conversely, bodies excrete sensations back into the environment. (p. 51)

This back-and-forthness of the body is therefore at once both concrete and transcendent. It is concrete at the pure, bodily level of sensation and it is transcendent in two senses: on the one hand, such sensation lies prior to the naming of experience and therefore becomes a 'transcendental condition of practical life' (Sparrow, 2013, p. 52), and on the other hand, sensation is precisely that which paradoxically enables a movement beyond the ego, the self and one's identity. This reading corresponds, I think, to the two kinds of transcendence Bergo (2014) has discussed in relation to Levinas's early and later work. As to the former, she writes: 'Levinas's early project approached transcendence in light of humans' irreducible urge to get past the limits of their physical and social situations. His transcendence is less transcendence-in-the-world than transcendence through and because of sensibility'. With respect to the later work, she notes that in *Otherwise in Being*, 'transcendence becomes transcendence-in-immanence before it is transcendence toward the other as untotalizable exteriority'. What I wish to suggest here is that reading Levinas as a philosopher of materiality allows us to posit the centrality of sensibility *both* in moving towards the Other in an act of transformation through which one becomes a responsible subject *and* in giving weight to the importance of unnamed (unnameable) experience as a condition for that movement to take place. Moreover, what focusing on sensibility and the body offer to both philosophy and education are a way of conceiving subjectivity in terms of its pliability and plasticity as it comes into contact with its environment.

Education Incarnate

What I have outlined here briefly in these pages is first that the newness of Levinas's philosophy emerges from reading him as a philosopher of materiality, which to my mind is a response not only to contemporary directions within philosophy, but also with the pedagogical concerns of transformation that we find within education. To theorise and practise education as though bodies were either incidental to its purpose or merely effects of the discourses that inform our teaching, is to dismiss too easily the ways in which bodies exceed the limits (we think) we are putting upon them. As Probyn suggests, bodies are not so readily contained, they seem to have their own 'logic' in responding to and in being immersed in their environments. Bodies perspire, blush, sneeze, sigh and breathe, and the skin tingles, twitches, pulses and produces even goose bumps. The sensational response to the environment is what constitutes our living flesh; the 'live subject' is one who is affecting and affected by its encounters with other material things. As such, subjects are plastic. 'The plastic subject is a dispositional subject, transitory and mutable. Its disposition is informed by its sensory environments and discernible in the sensations it can endure and produce at any given moment ...' (Sparrow, 2013, p. 56). And as we have seen it is this malleability occasioned by a vulnerability to the Other that enables the ethical subject to emerge in Levinas's work. It is precisely our susceptibility to the Other, and our capacity to respond to the Other as someone in her own right, outside of my perception of her, where Levinas locates ethics. The ethical subject is a responsible subject, transcending the 'givenness' of the ego, allowing the immediacy of sensibility to be experienced, without being named or categorised. Plasticity, it seems to me, is the very nature of the Levinasian ethical subject.

Plasticity, and the significance of the immediacy of sensibility on Levinas's terms, is also what I would call eminently pedagogical. For me, it is the alteration of the self in an act of 'sensible transcendence' that captures what it is we are talking about when we talk about the transformative possibilities of education. That is, whatever kind of change we are advocating through our educational projects (better citizens, freer persons, critical thinkers, empathic and caring individuals) is reliant upon the actual sensations experienced by bodies in encounters with their ever-changing environment. There is no citizen, person, thinker or individual that is not a living entity made of flesh and blood. Transformations, whether they occur through an engagement with ideas or gestures or things, are never purely cognitive events, but always accompanied by concrete effects which in turn condition the lived environment we then experience anew.[5] Levinas's bold move was to turn this pedagogical (transformative) moment of subjectivity, with all its sensations, into the very condition of responsibility.

LEVINAS AND THE PHILOSOPHY OF EDUCATION

But what are we to do with a view of education that is incarnate at the level of the sensate body? It is one thing to theorise sensations and affects, analysing how they come into being, seeking to understand the place they have in our personal stories or cultural narratives, but it is wholly other thing to simply 'let' them exist and see that existence as valuable in its own right. That is, while there is a need for analysing the guilt white students might feel in confronting their own privilege or the rage that women experience in the face of continued discrimination, there is also a need for accepting that the bodily sensations of guilt and rage are nonetheless living experiences that without our intention circulate in, around and through us. This is not a call for anti-intellectualism—quite the opposite in fact. Instead, it is a plea for acknowledging the significance of the unnameable, uncategorisable aspects of sensation that Levinas was at pains to articulate through his poetic renderings of subjectivity. By making room for the directness of experience and the immediacy of sensibility as central aspect of classroom life, could we not then begin to practise a kind of attunement, an orientation to the unpredictable qualities of bodily responses? After all, if we follow the spirit of Levinas, is it not in and through my body that my responsibility begins?

Disclosure statement

No potential conflict of interest was reported by the author.

Notes

1. See Todd (2014) for a depiction of pedagogy as that which involves the transformation of the self—a transformation which involves both the body and spirit.
2. Some authors draw on Karen Barad's work in physics to speak about intra-action and not only interaction. For a discussion of the differences, see Hekman (2010), pp. 72–78.
3. One notable exception she makes is O'Farrell *et al.*'s edited volume entitled, *Taught Bodies* (2000).
4. Indeed, Sparrow takes Levinas to task for failing to adequately account for the phenomenological encounter with the face in all its specificity and links this failure to systems of racial discrimination. Although I am sympathetic to many of his points, I do think that there is a broader issue at stake that Sparrow does not fully address. This is the issue of singularity itself. From the critique raised against Levinas by feminists such as Luce Irigaray and Adriana Caverero, the point is that Levinas's subject dissolves too easily into a generalisation of the other, as one who has no (sexual) specificity to contend with. Indeed, these critiques fit the work of other philosophers of uniqueness, such as Jean-Luc Nancy, who are also depicted as missing out on the radical singularity of a unique being in making claims about 'beings' and 'others' in general.
5. For an interesting discussion of this recursion and the emergence of consciousness as an interactive relation, see Noë (2010) and Thompson (2007). Both authors write at the intersection of philosophy, cognitive science and neuroscience and examine the plasticity of human organisms and their environments.

LEVINAS AND THE PHILOSOPHY OF EDUCATION

References

Ahmed, S. (2004). *The cultural politics of emotion*. Edinburgh: Edinburgh University Press.

Atterton, P. (2012). Facing animals. In W. Edelglass, J. Hatley, & C. Diem (Eds.), *Facing nature: Levinas and environmental thought* (pp. 25–40). Pittsburgh, PA: Duquesne University Press.

Bergo, B. (2014). Emmanuel Levinas. In E. N. Zalta (Ed.), *The Stanford encyclopedia of philosophy* (Spring 2014 ed.). Retrieved June 14, 2014, from http://plato.stanford.edu/archives/spr2014/entries/levinas/

Bernasconi, R. (2010). Globalization and world hunger: Kant and Levinas. In P. Atterton & M. Calarco (Eds.), *Radicalizing Levinas* (pp. 69–84). Albany, NY: SUNY Press.

Biesta, G. (2006). *Beyond learning*. Boulder: Paradigm.

Calarco, M. (2010). Faced by animals. In P. Atterton & M. Calarco (Eds.), *Radicalizing Levinas* (pp. 113–133). Albany, NY: SUNY Press.

Chinnery, A. (2003). Aesthetics of surrender: Levinas and the disruption of agency in moral education. *Studies in Philosophy and Education, 22*, 5–17.

Davies, B. (2009). Difference and differentiation. In B. Davies & S. Gannon (Eds.), *Pedagogical encounters* (pp. 17–30). New York, NY: Peter Lang.

Edelglass, W. (2012). Rethinking responsibility in an age of anthropogenic climate catastrophe. In W. Edelglass, J. Hatley, & C. Diem (Eds.), *Facing nature: Levinas and environmental thought* (pp. 209–228). Pittsburgh, PA: Duquesne University Press.

Egéa-Kuehne, D. (Ed.). (2008). *Levinas and education: At the intersection of faith and reason*. New York, NY: Routledge.

Gallop, J. (1995). *Pedagogy: A question of impersonation*. Bloomington: Indiana University Press.

Gallop, J. (1997). *Feminist accused of sexual harrassment*. Durham, NC: Duke University Press.

Hekman, S. (2010). *The material of knowledge: Feminist disclosures*. Bloomington: Indiana University Press.

Joldersma, C. W. (2002). *Pedagogy of the other: A Levinasian approach to the teacher–student relationship*. In S. Rice (Ed.), *Philosophy of education society yearbook 2001* (pp. 181–188). Urbana, IL: Philosophy of Education Society-University of Illinois.

Kodelja, Z. (2008). Autonomy and heteronomy. In D. Egéa-Kuehne (Ed.), *Levinas and education* (pp. 186–197). London: Routledge.

Lenz Taguchi, H. (2011). Investigating learning, participation and becoming in early childhood practices with a relational materialist approach. *Global Studies of Childhood, 1*, 36–50.

Levinas, E. (1969). *Totality and infinity*. (A. Lingis, Trans.). Pittsburgh, PA: Duquesne University Press.

Levinas, E. (1987). *Time and the other*. (R. A. Cohen, Trans.). Pittsburgh, PA: Duquesne University Press.

Levinas, E. (1998). *Otherwise than being or beyond essence*. (A. Lingis, Trans.). Pittsburgh, PA: Duquesne University Press.

Llewelyn, J. (2010). Pursuing Levinas and Ferry toward a newer and more democratic ecological order. In P. Atterton & M. Calarco (Eds.), *Radicalizing levinas* (pp. 95–112). Albany, NY: SUNY Press.

Noë, A. (2010). *Out of our heads: Why you are not your brain, and other lessons from the biology of consciousness*. New York, NY: Hill and Wang.

O'Farrell, C., Meadmore, D., McWilliam, E., & Symes, C. (2000). *Taught bodies*. New York, NY: Peter Lang.

Perpich, D. (2008). *The ethics of Emmanuel Levinas*. Stanford, CA: Stanford University Press.

Probyn, E. (2004). Teaching bodies: Affects in the classroom. *Body and Society, 10*, 21–43.

Säfström, C. A. (2003). Teaching otherwise. *Studies in Philosophy and Education, 22*, 19–29.

Simmons, J. A. (2012). Toward a relational model of anthropocentrism: A Levinasian approach to the ethics of climate change. In W. Edelglass, J. Hatley, & C. Diem (Eds.), *Facing nature: Levinas and environmental thought* (pp. 229–252). Pittsburgh, PA: Duquesne University Press.

Sparrow, T. (2013). *Levinas unhinged*. Winchester: Zero Books.

Standish, P. (2008). Levinas and the language of the curriculum. In D. Egéa-Kuehne (Ed.), *Levinas and education* (pp. 56–65). London: Routledge.

Strhan, A. (2009). *The very subjection of the subject: Levinas, heteronomy and the philosophy of education*. Paper presented at the PESGB conference, Oxford, UK.

Taylor, C. A., & Invinson, G. (2013). Special Issue: Material feminisms: New directions for education. *Gender and Education, 25*, 665–670.

Thompson, E. (2007). *Mind in life: Biology, phenomenology, and the sciences of mind*. Cambridge, MA: Harvard University Press.

Todd, S. (2003). *Learning from the other: Levinas, psychoanalysis and ethical possibilities in education*. Albany, NY: SUNY Press.

Todd, S. (2008). Welcoming and difficult learning: Reading Levinas with education. In D. Egéa-Kuehne (Ed.), *Levinas and education* (pp. 170–185). London: Routledge.

Todd, S. (2014). Between body and spirit: The Liminality of pedagogical relationships. *Journal of Philosophy of Education, 48*, 231–245.

Winter, C. (2014). Curriculum knowledge, justice, relations: The schools white paper (2010) in England. *Journal of Philosophy of Education, 48*, 276–292.

Taking Responsibility into all Matter: Engaging Levinas for the climate of the 21st Century

BETSAN MARTIN

Abstract

This paper works with Levinasian thought to ask how principles of responsibility can be engaged for the twenty-first century crisis of climate destabilization, and other matters of injustice and exploitation. A case is made for extending an ethics of responsibility from a human-centered view to include humans as interdependent with nature. After a selective review of responsibility as inaugurating an ontology of otherwise-than-being, *consideration is given to the phenomenology of the face-to-face relation and to notions of a teaching relation, to knowledge and to Levinas' notion of justice, in line with the philosophical and educational interests of this journal. The prospect of society constituted on responsibility is brought to life in a brief reference to Māori society and indigenous thought. An interpretation of quantum theory is also introduced because of its analogies with the inter-related world view of indigenous thought. These all point to relationality which antecedes the ontology of* being. *While much is made of Levinas' work on the face, this paper argues that it is in principles of ethics that break with totality, and Levinas' notions of transcendence and infinity rather than the face* per se *that enable us to broaden the scope of reference for Levinasian ethics. Levinasian ethics question the stronghold of liberal humanistic goals in educational vision, and open a horizon of the shared destiny of humans and nature—an 'eco-pedagogy.' The paper draws these threads together to consider their relevance to education for sustainability.*

Responsibility grows in importance as the life of freedom discovers itself to be unjust. (Levinas, 1987, p. 58)

LEVINAS AND THE PHILOSOPHY OF EDUCATION

Introduction

We may do nothing better than work with the ethics of Emmanuel Levinas for responses to the precarious matters of our time.

For this paper, freedom and justice in the opening citation are touchstones for selective critique of Cartesian metaphysics of binary opposition and liberalism, of which freedom is a central tenet. These are central to Levinas' critique and the basis of his oeuvre for ethics beyond being, as responsibility *for* the Other.

This is a fundamental shift from *being* which is characterized by self-interest (egoism) and freedom (from constraint). An enclosed, individualistic notion of identity characterizes the liberal humanist and industrial project (Hall, 1986). The humanist foundations of economic liberalism exclude environmental ecology from its system of accounts, and tend to regard an account of environmental impacts as a barrier to economic progress. The exclusion of the environment is put in question by the calamity of climate change. As we turn from the precepts of liberalism, we find that collaboration, integration, and relational ethics are regarded as being at the heart of the transition to sustainability (Berkes, Colding, & Folke, 2003).

Levinas considers the freedom and self-interest embedded in liberal traditions to be constituted on violence—a power relation of mastery identified in the culture–nature split and subject–object, same–other binaries. Taking us far beyond critique of liberalism and ontology, Levinas offers an exposé of the relational condition and the ethical capacity of the human person.

The driving force of Levinas's critique is to offer an alternative to the violence of western metaphysics; it makes a paradigm shift away from ontological subjectivity premised on subordinating the other, the ontology of 'being', to ethics constituted in responsibility for the Other, the stranger, the neighbor. This is an ontology to escape the egoism of being, of being enclosed in individual identity and agency, by exposing the human condition as nested within a relational system (Levinas 'Transcendence and Height' in Peperzak, Critchley and Bernasconi, 1996a). An interest of this paper is to deepen Levinas' premise of a preconscious relationality with a venture into an idea of responsibility as the ground of all becoming.

Levinas' claim to relationality as the primordial condition of human life is taken to a demanding register through the notion of responsibility. Responsibility is understood not as blame, but as service, and is brought to life in the face-to-face encounter between two. In this modality, ethics is shifted from an individual morality to an account of identity and justice wholly premised on response to an Other, whom he consistently denotes as the neighbor and the stranger.

Responsibility for Levinas, opens in a gesture of welcome, and in sharing bread and water. Welcome and the offer of hospitality are tied to the source of these provisions: land, water, air, and light. The paper works with the motif of hospitality to venture beyond the human-centered locus of Levinas to draw out a notion of the interdependence of humans and nature.

Levinas' articulation of responsibility as welcome to the Other is human centered because it seeks to supplant human violence—violence as objectification or mastery over another. In arguing for radical responsibility to disrupt the sovereign self in its ontological totality, he paves the way for a new ontology, beyond *being per se*. Levinas' ontology of a relational, responsible 'I' as being-*for*-the-other, or *Otherwise than Being*, opens the prospect of a new order of justice arising from an ethics of responsibility *for* the Other (Levinas, 1996c).

Levinas' thinking serves as the home, and also the host for this discussion. As such, it is a place for hospitality offered to neighbors and strangers of thought. Hosting is working *with* his thinking in new settings, invoking a willingness to be taught from different knowledge systems.

In countries with colonial histories such as New Zealand, Western social systems and world views are in an uneasy juxtaposition, as well as in fertile exchange with those of Māori and Pacific peoples. This paper does not pursue the obvious Levinasian argument of the violence of colonization. Rather, the interest is on relations of obligation and hospitality, which are paramount in Māori society, and have extraordinary resonance with Levinasian interests. In Māori (and Pacific) indigenous societies relationships are interwoven with all life forms, and there is no distinction between animate and inanimate categories characteristic of western understandings of the natural world. Quantum mechanics, as interpreted by Karen Barad, offers a non-human-centered world view with an approach to responsibility which extends to all phenomena and so has resonance with indigenous thought.

Indigenous systems offer a world where obligation is the source of sociality and is a reference for justice. Obligation should not be fully equated with responsibility. While responsibility generally has an element of choice, obligation is bestowed, even compelled, and it is implicit in traditional values. This seems close to Levinas' idea of the inescapable demand of the Other.

Indigenous thought should not be equated with sustainability even though there are similar interests. Sustainability is a discourse intended to correct the sectorial divisions of industrial economies and achieve integration of social, environmental, and economic systems, whereas indigenous systems are cosmological, intergenerational, and spiritual in scope and cannot be confined to sustainability agendas (Tunks, 2013).

A quite different account of responsibility is found in Karen Barad's interpretation of quantum physics (Barad, 2003). Barad allows us to see intelligence and responsiveness in all matter, for which she uses the all encompassing term, phenomena. Phenomena refers to humans, plants, animals, and all forms of matter and thus provides a different pathway to collapsing the nature–culture split.

I find that this has resonance with indigenous thought in that it assumes all matter is living, dynamic, and responsive, and it enhances the principle that all of life is interdependent and in dynamic process. In the tentative, exploratory, and brief reference to quantum physics, I explore Barad's inference that responsibility is the ground of all becoming, and suggest a link with Levinas' interests in a relational interactive mode that is *other than being*. Responsibility as responsiveness is a touchstone for linking with Levinas' notion of primordial relationality and its expression in responsibility.

Returning to Levinas' societal ethics and his use of the term *le tiers* to denote the presence of all (human) others, the paper discusses an expanded notion of responsibility as a reference for justice.

An expanded view of humans as interdependent with nature has profound implications for teaching and learning and knowledge development. Although education for sustainability may seem strange and far from Levinas' concerns, it is an educational discourse which holds the possibility of an ethical account of human interdependence with nature.

Education in this mode takes us on a trajectory of cultivating knowledge of interdependence and relationality to curb the 'injustice' inherent in individualized freedom; it supports a turn toward an imperative of responsibility.

I am interested in asking how an ethics of responsibility comes to life in the twenty-first century? This is a time when we are facing the destruction of the fabric of life as we know it. We are acknowledging that humans and nature are interdependent, and jointly part of one planetary ecosystem. What forms of social systems are needed to stabilize the climate and address the explosive symptoms of social alienation? In what ways does Levinas provide some guidance?

Levinas: The Face and the Scope of Responsibility

With an interest in taking Levinas beyond the human-centered focus of much of his work, we can take some of the touchstones: transcendence, infinity, alterity, and the dictum 'thou shalt not kill' and ask 'to what or to whom does this apply?' To humans, animals, fish, ecosystems? When Levinas works with the motif of the face-to-face relation to signify the relation with the Other as ethics, the 'face' is usually read as a human face.

Commentators such as Diane Perpich (2008, p. 168 ff.) and John Llewelyn (1991) have examined Levinasian ethics for extending it beyond the human to animals and nature, or the living world. That discussion includes whether consciousness and language are necessary conditions of ethical responsibility, and much discussion turns on the meaning of the face, and whether the face, in Levinas, is only a human face, or can be other faces, such as a snake or a cat, that command a response.

I propose that the face of the Other is the wrong locus for interpreting responsibility. The focus for responsibility is with the Same, with *me*. The face brings *my* exposure to the Other, it is where I encounter the infinite, that which is beyond the grasp of understanding. The Other disturbs *my* interested freedom.

In my view, the focus on the phenomenon of the face is an incorrect locus for these questions of responsibility, even though they are interesting in the light of power of the motif of the face. I will follow some discussion of the face for its phenomenological importance. When the face-to-face relation is coded as 'the face', it tends to focus on the Other, and the impact on *being* is lost. The 'face' as the Other, when over scrutinized, loses its quality of alterity and becomes an other, an object.

Levinas' himself gives varying meanings of the face, an ambiguity of which Perpich recognizes:

> the face is both perceptible and imperceptible, that it appears but is not reducible to its visual or perceptible form. It is a structure that ... overflows the determinate meaning that it none-the-less has, that is both open to my

appropriation and forever resisting that grasp with a "no" .... (Perpich, 2008, p. 171)

In his later essay *Peace and Proximity, precariousness* is the condition of ethics (Levinas, 1996b, p. 167). Sensitivity to precariousness generates responsibility for the Other. The phenomenon of the face of the Other creates an impossible demand, an infinite summons to respond that is beyond my capacity to fulfill.

> The ethical I is subjectivity precisely insofar as it kneels before the other, sacrificing its own liberty to the more primordial call of the other. For me, the freedom of the subject is not the highest or primary value. The heteronomy of our response to the human other, or to God as absolutely other precedes the autonomy of our subjective freedom. As soon as I acknowledge that it is 'I' who am responsible, I accept that my freedom is anteceded by an obligation to the other. (Levinas, 1986, p. 27)

Being-for-the other, which Levinas also terms *proximity*, is a severe sacrificial demand of the Other upon *me* which reaches to the extent of giving of bread from one's own mouth. This is an usurping of freedom and self-interest par excellence.

With the undecidability of Levinas himself on the subject of the face, he goes back on this idea of the face as openness to reassert his central theme of the infinity of the Other. He writes:

> We cannot even say that the face is an opening, for this would be to make it relative to environmental plenitude'. (Levinas, 1996c, p. 10)

These are difficult passages for an introductory section, but it conveys the central theme of his ethics in which the Other cannot be reduced to *my* consciousness, is unknowable and beyond my grasp.

In order to argue for responsibility beyond the human, Perpich moves to Levinas' work on justice and idea of society as the realm where humans are mandated to make decisions for the human and nonhuman spheres. This argument is a major step toward the thesis that all arenas—human, environment, climate—are fitting concerns for justice in the Levinasian sense. However, this view does not reconcile justice in the social sphere with the face-to-face relation. Critchley (1992) achieves this reconciliation with his notion of the double structure of justice discussed later in this paper.

Radical Responsibility

Levinas' conception of the relational condition of human life does not rest with understanding the identity of the face; the face of the Other is an enigma. The 'Same', 'myself' is the site of transformation, where tension with the agency of the ontological subject as *being* is experienced.

> [O]ntology is not accomplished in the triumph of human beings over their condition but in the very tension where this condition is assumed. (Levinas, 1996c, p. 3)

LEVINAS AND THE PHILOSOPHY OF EDUCATION

In classical ontology identity is achieved through self assertion and by diminishing the other. Levinas refers to this as the 'triumph' of mastery and the violence of assimilation. In seeking an alternative to this violence:

> Can the Same welcome the Other, not by giving itself to the Other as a theme, (that is to say as being) but by putting itself in question? (Levinas, 1996b, p. 16)

The question is further elaborated:

> Does not this putting in question occur precisely when the Other has nothing in common with me, when the other is wholly Other, that is a human Other (Autre)? When through the nakedness and destitution of his defenseless eyes, he forbids murder and paralyzes my impetuous freedom. (ibid.)

The putting in question of 'myself', the sovereign self, is a questioning that is prior to choice and intention. It is not a conscious act of will; it is a fundamental unsettling of will, intention and consciousness, and of liberty. The Other, whom Levinas denotes as the Stranger and the Neighbor, interpolates 'me' and in this moment, presents responsibility.

The startling account of responsibility as the condition of being in hostage to the Other, is an example of where the severity of Levinas' argument takes hold. The face is a motif for openness, for exposure to the external world through the senses. The face symbolizes a break with the idea of an enclosed entity, a totality of being. Levinas argues that the response it elicits is the basis of empathy which he says is the condition of transference from 'by the other' to 'for the other.'

> It is through the condition of being hostage that there can be in the world pity, compassion, pardon, proximity .... The unconditionality of being hostage is not the limit case of solidarity, but the condition for all solidarity. (Levinas, 2009, p. 117)

Perpich largely resolves the question of violation of the self as a hostage to the Other with her notion of the moral force of responsibility, a force which is inescapable at the level of conscience. Although a response can be refused, the 'call' of another cannot be escaped. (Perpich, 2008; in 'Responsibility: the Infinity of the Demand' pp. 78–123) This is an argument which makes the impossibility of the demand of responsibility intelligible and comfortable. It destroys the impact of disturbance that the Other presents. In my view, responsibility at the level of conscience de-radicalizes the paradigmatic shift that Levinas launches, and lessens the impact of the shift from ontological egoism to responsibility. As Levinas clearly says, responsibility is engagement (Levinas, 1996c).

There is power in the extremity of his argument, in the shock of extreme accountability for the Other. To be a hostage means that freedom is subverted by responsibility. To be hostage to another exposes the situation of human community and solidarity where welcome and hospitality are realized.

Therefore, the other does not limit our freedom in a physical or mathematical sense. Freedom is unmasked as injustice and summoned to change the exercise of violence into goodness and hospitality. (De Boer, 1986, p. 93)

Responsibility is performed in sensible, material actions befitting the nearness, proximity of 'my' neighbor and the height of the Other who is Strange—wholly Other. In mediating the face-to-face relation, my response in language is a mode of speaking which escapes the confines of ontology and the judgment of reason—the saying, the lively attentive response, gives significance to the Other and does not produce the Other as an object.

The face is a phenomenological method for signifying the senses and material plane which open and bind us to the Other. It signifies consciousness that can be expressed as will and as receptiveness. The aliveness of the face and of communication are accomplished through air—in the breath. Food and water as sustenance for the body is taken through the mouth, human connection with light and sound are concentrated in the face.

Can we extend the motif of hospitality to give us a practical ethics of responsibility across the human and non-human? To offer water and food might take us to the supermarket, but beyond that it takes us to land and food production and to access to food. To provide grain and meat implicates us in agriculture and the sustainability of land management and the risk of precarious, exploitative, or unprecautionary industrial agriculture.

Do we want to offer GM food? To offer clean water, are we obliged to safeguard waterways? Does the offer of fish imply the need to be embedded in systems of custodianship for rivers and ocean ecosystems and fish habitats? Does Levinas offer an ethics of response to human exploitation and the precarious state of ecosystems?

A Teaching Relation and Infinite Unknowing

If the Other is to be recognized in his or her alterity, the relationship becomes a teaching relation with a position of being willing to be taught. Again, this idea rests on the self, the Same, not the Other.

The ethical relation is characterized as a teaching relation because no assumption can be made about another based on the self. Working with the motifs of depth and height, we find that the ethical relation is produced by teaching and listening:

> The Other, qua Other ... has the face of the poor, the widow, and the orphan, and at the same time, of the master called to invest and justify my freedom. The relation that is established—the relationship of teaching, of mastery, of transitivity—is language and is produced in the speaker who consequently himself faces. (Levinas, 1969, p. 251)

Now freedom is recast as *my* opportunity to respond, displacing the idea that responsibility imposes a constraint on my freedom. The 'I' as the free and knowing subject of philosophy, with its 'comprehensive claims to mastery' (Critchley, 1992, p. 8) is undone on the positioning of one as willing to be taught.

It is therefore to receive the Other beyond the capacity of the I, which means exactly: to have the idea of infinity. But this also means: to be taught. The relation with the other, or conversation, is a nonallergic relation, an ethical relation: but inasmuch as it is welcomed this conversation is a teaching relation. (Levinas, 1969, p. 51)

We find in Levinas an idea of unknowing, of life that cannot be enclosed within the limits of human consciousness, nor in the temporality of presence. The importance of the infinite is that there is a realm that escapes knowing, that is in excess of human cognition.

For Levinas, knowledge is the realm of the other because it is exterior to the human person. The acquisition of knowledge to achieve consciousness and identity has the same risk of objectification.

Knowledge is a relation of the *Same* with the *Other* in which the Other is reduced to the Same and divested of its strangeness … the other is no longer other as such, the other is already appropriated, already *mine*. (Levinas, 1996e, p. 151)

This view of knowledge can be transposed to the idea that *I am responsible, therefore I become*; it is an ouvre contra Descarte's knowing subject which Levinas refers to as the adequation of knowledge with the knower, or appropriation. In the ontology of *being*, it is knowledge subjected to the grasp; it is a further instance of totality. The theme of transcendence, of the Other as infinite, always beyond the grasp of my consciousness, lends itself to the new consciousness and a new order of society, and as will be proposed, a society of sustainability.

Justice

The glimpse at impossible, inescapable, and non-representable responsibility is intended to disrupt ontological systems at the subjective and societal levels. While the impossible demand of Levinas' ethics might be extreme and impractical, it needs to be considered in the context of his elaboration of justice—the principle of responsibility in the relation between two, is a relation in the context of community and society. This is not a private relation, unexposed to communal bonds, as Simon Critchley importantly observes (Critchley, 1992, p. 222). The face-to-face relation simultaneously encompasses *le tiers*, the third person representing society in general.

The way leads from responsibility to problems …. The extraordinary commitment of the Other with regard to the third party calls for control, to the search for justice, to society and the State, to comparison and possession, and to commerce and philosophy, and, outside of anarchy, to the search for principle. Philosophy is this measure brought to the infinity of the being-for-the-other of proximity, and it is like the wisdom of love. (Levinas, 2009, p. 161)

In this sociality, ethics gives birth to justice that emerges from relational responsibility. This prospect is vastly different from the premise that sociality is founded of a war of all against all with institutions that are designed to protect self-interest and independence with attendant values of freedom and private property.

There is a certain pragmatism in Levinas' view of justice, as he acknowledges a re-inscription of ontology in the order of sociality with co-citizenship in a shared social order. However, this is not the same ontology that privileges freedom and self-interest; it now embodies principles from ethics in the Levinasian sense.

> Out of representation is produced the order of justice moderating or measuring the substitution of me for the other .... Justice requires the contemporaneousness of representation. It is thus that the neighbor becomes visible, and, looked at, presents himself, and there is also justice for me. The saying is fixed in a said, is written, becomes a book, law, science. (Levinas, 2009, pp. 158–159)

And further

> The equality of all is borne by my inequality, the surplus of my duties over my rights. The forgetting of self moves justice. (Levinas, 2009, p. 159)

The forgetting of self now becomes a principle of citizenship and justice that generates the capacity for judgment and questioning at the public and political arenas. The face-to-face relation in play in sociality stays open to advocacy for justice–open to the disruptive interpolation of the prophetic voice (Levinas, 2009, pp. 149–152). The prophetic role is the responsibility to represent situations of vulnerability, the precariousness to which all are susceptible. This is where the notion of *le tiers* signifies responsibility to the specific Other transposed into all others.

Without a reading of the transposition of the face-to-face ethical relation to justice, and to teaching, the extreme summons to responsibility is untenable. Education theorists come to an impasse when considering whether the ego-less subject can be realized. This article is not the place for further discussion on subjectivity and identity, but one might ask whether ego/ego-less are the only avenues for human realization of identity, and whether self esteem and meaning can be achieved altruistically. For Levinas, meaning, value, and identity are achieved in responsibility.

The possibilities for cultivating an ethics of 'for the other' in teaching practice, as discussed by Zhao (2012), become realizable when mediated through 'justice.' Cultivation of a response of welcome as an event in the social order and an expression of 'justice' offers a form of personhood that is supported by institutional and social arrangements. In other words, a process of word (of welcome) and world, or *saying* and sociality in co-production.

The impetus to bring an ethics of responsibility into public life is taking place beyond the confines of philosophical deliberation. It is taking place in law, in comparative cultural studies and education and sustainability to bring the principle of responsibility into public life (Calame, 2012; Grinlinton & Taylor, 2011, pp. 1–20; Hoskins, 2010; Martin, 2014; Sizoo, 2010).

Analogies with Indigenous Societal Systems

Levinasian thinking of a preconscious relationality and responsibility marks a progression in western metaphysics that is already present in indigenous cultures, and indeed in other traditional societies. In contrast to the western philosophical tradition where identity is anchored in the Cartesian dualistic system and achieved through the self–other relation, indigenous identity arises from land and ancestral genealogical relations.

This thought on responsibility and relational ethics is moving toward what is already understood in the indigenous worldview of Te Ao Māori. Using the metaphor of woven universe, Charles Te Ahukaramu Royal and Māori Marsden articulate an integrative metaphysics which is constitutive of tikanga (law and custom) and associated knowledge and practice (Royal, 2003; Royal & Martin, 2010).

Te Kawehau Hoskins reflects 'Indigenous peoples, continue to remember and articulate a discourse of responsibility and obligation to others and to natural environments' (Hoskins, Martin, & Humphries, 2011, p. 23).

> Māori for example see themselves as part of a familial web in which humans are junior siblings to other species beings and forms of life. People therefore don't understand themselves as exercising knowledge over the natural world but as existing always already *inside* or *as* relationships. (Hoskins et al., 2011, p. 23)

In an indigenous worldview, the human world, known as the world of light, is but one of many dimensions of an interconnected cosmology. The world of ancestors and genealogical connections thread their way through multiple dimensions of this cosmology to an originating burst of energy. Kinship between all life forms (of which humans are one manifestation) and across these dimensions is shared through the notion of hau, breath or wind. In the words of distinguished Professor Anne Salmond

> Here there is no radical disjuncture between mind and matter, thought and emotion, subject and object, the ideal and the real. Because everything is animated by hau tupu and hau ora, the winds of growth and life, including objects and people ... animate and inanimate phenomena are not distinguished. (Salmond, 2012, p. 120)

The notion of breath and wind, hau, is linked etymologically with I, denoting a person. The word for I in Māori is ahau, suggesting a manifestation of ancestors in 'me,' this person. A person in the here and now of this world (of light) is the living face of an ancestor for whom he or she speaks. In this sense, a person now might incarnate the face of a one who has passed on, or another entity—an extinct bird, such as a huia, or a fish or a dog in their ancestral lineage of the land of their origin, in order to give expression to a point of view needed in the present time. The hau, the winds of life and growth moving across time and space and all matter give further possibilities for responsibility and the face.

There are analogies here with Levinas' notion of sociality, such as the face-to-face relation and obligations of hospitality that suggest compelling links between these different systems of thought and tradition and give a glimpse of sociality, politics, and decision-making founded on relational ethics (Hoskins, 2010). A differentiating feature is that Levinas is seeking to re-orient violence within a system, and bring principles of relationality to correct the structure of the social order.

The management of violence is part of all social systems. Indigenous systems are not a panacea to totalitarian or liberal systems and the violence that Levinas points to. Rather, they suggest a different possibility from the hegemony of liberalism. They also suggest a compelling synergy with the dynamics of quantum physics.

The very selective reading of Karen Barad's account of quantum dynamics is explored here and builds on indigenous thought, with which it has some analogies, to bring a further account of responsibility. This is not a human-centered responsibility, but it extends the scope of responsibility as a condition of all matter.

Ethics, Knowledge, and Quantum Considerations

Barad (2003) gives a view of responsibility as constitutive of all inter-actions between phenomena. This is a term that includes all forms of matter, it does not distinguish between animate and inanimate, human and non-human. It marks a radical shift from human-centered to an eco-centric understanding of the world.

On this view, Barad suggests we view humans as one manifestation of electrons and particles amongst all phenomena, and thus she takes ethics into the realm of all matter.

> "[H]umans" refers to phenomena, not [as] independent entities with inherent properties but rather beings in their differential becoming. (Barad, 2003, p. 818)

The quantum field is composed of particles, field, and the void. The void is not vacuous, but a space of virtual particle activity—activity which is not confined to 'presence.' This means the activity of particles cannot be measured in time as we know it. They are simultaneously 'being and non-being.' Point particles are inseparable from the void, and are intrinsic to it. Point particles are able to interact with each other through the electromagnetic field to create infinite possibilities of particles becoming phenomena.

In this view, all encounters of matter create a response in one and another. The term intra-action conveys the mutual and multiple interplays of phenomena; intra-action moves matter to the register of ethics by the interpretation that all intra-actions are constituted in 'response-ability.'

Quantum mechanics therefore introduces a dynamic view of all matter. Particles and electrons can move from one energy level to another without traveling, without being in between levels. Time and space are reconfigured: the impacts of a passed event can be removed after the event—not erased—and a trace of evidence remains in the present as testimony to a past action. Encounters between all forms of matter produce infinite new expression of matter, life is reproduced and evolves into endless new differentiations which also remain connected, entangled, intertwined, never fully differentiated from their source.

LEVINAS AND THE PHILOSOPHY OF EDUCATION

The observed difference, or the distinctiveness of phenomena, is not one of complete otherness/individuation because matter is always already entangled with or open to the other. Humans and all matter emerge through specific intra-actions in and with the world; and this gives rise to the idea that we are responsible for the relationalities through which we are constituted. Therefore, we are already responsible because we are part of others from which we take new form. An 'ethics of worlding' rather than a humanist ethics! (Barad, 2007).

Identities/phenomena are relational, they do not exist as fully different individuals. The difference we observe is simply an expression of differentiation with an underlying entanglement.

How do Quantum Dynamics Link to Levinas and Ethics?

While this paper draws on a limited reference to Barad's dynamics of matter, the similarities with Levinas are apparent. Levinas' exposure of the fault of the idea of the ontological subject as a distinct agential individual subject striving for presence is substantiated by Barad's account of the relational condition of matter. Usurping presence, and claiming responsibility as the ground of all becoming are shared by Levinas and Barad.

Interpretation of Levinas in the light of these wider references to responsibility has led me back to his essay 'Is Ontology Fundamental?' (Levinas, 1996c) Levinasian ontology means to be embedded in existence as such, as intra-active with all that he or she depends on and offers for life. It is lived in performativity. This marks a rupture in western thought which has been mired in intellectualism divorced from engagement in the material conditions of life. The now well-known importance of context for interpreting meaning and value is another way of recognizing that a person's situation, their 'facticity of temporal existence' gives shape, meaning, and expression to thought and existence. In the next passage, it can be readily seen that to be engaged in philosophy and in ethics means to take action, to commit, to be engaged.

> The return to the original themes of philosophy [proceeds] from a radical attention given to the urgent preoccupations of the moment. The abstract question of the meaning of being and the question of the present hour spontaneously reunite ....

> To think is no longer to contemplate but to commit oneself, to be engulfed by that which one thinks, to be involved. This is the dramatic event of being-in-the-world. (Levinas, 1996c, pp. 3–4)

A radical engagement in the world is fully at one with an ontology of not reducing the Other to my consciousness, to the grasp of comprehension. If ethics is responsibility, it is activated in the relation of one-for-another in society. Thus the principle of responsibility of openness is at work at the level of society. Indigenous forms of identity and society reveal the lived reality of social systems which arise from obligation in all dimensions—the 'world of light' and the worlds beyond knowing.

LEVINAS AND THE PHILOSOPHY OF EDUCATION

When Levinas says 'we are responsible beyond our intentions' (ibid., p. 4), he may not have had in mind the global dimensions of some concerns raised here, he was speaking out of the enormity of the holocaust. Climate change is a human-induced systemic disturbance being set in motion over unprecedented timescales and beyond the known intentions of the collective impacts of polluting the atmosphere. In this case, it is nature that is calling *us* into question. Nature is the Other. It exposes the consequences of the failure to account for human life interwoven with the living world.

Being open and intra-active is a condition of all matter—plants, rocks, water, creatures, fabric, plastic—and these are qualities and dynamics that draw together the diverse threads here in recognition of intra-activity in all dimensions. The ethical demand of Levinas can be brought to bear on the condition of openness.

> Does not the fact of being is "open" belong to the very fact of its being? Our concrete existence is interpreted in terms of its entry into the "openness" of being in general. We exist in a circuit of understanding with reality. (ibid., p. 5)

When discussing disturbance that the Other brings to signify the break with the enclosed notion of being, Levinas says with extreme brevity 'correlation is broken' (Levinas, 1996d, p. 77). To me, this is the heart of his ethics. While the face may provide a platform, a phenomenology for his argument, it is the principle of non-correlation that allows the concept of responsibility to be taken to a wider scope than the human Other.

In Levinasian terms, the face is a phenomenological device to elicit ethics, to expose *my* responsibility and the attributes of openness, alterity, and so on. It is the response of responsibility that is important, more than the enigma of the face. With this view in mind, it is unnecessary to contest the identity of the face. The Other to be welcomed may indeed be a stranger of another order than the human. The essence of Levinas is to break with totality of *being*, to subvert freedom, and to ensure an ever-open horizon of the infinite to guard against non-enclosure in *being*, the source of violence.

We see that the human capacity for violence to the human other is of the same order as violating the fabric of life. To pollute the air is to poison ourselves and all forms of life and matter. In indigenous terms, we are interfering with 'hau', the animating principle of life with unknowable consequences. Levinas draws us to the means of *becoming otherwise* to create a sociality that comprehends a quantum view of interconnectedness. These two dimensions invoke a new discourse of an *oeconomy* founded on responsibility (Calame, 2009), which recognizes responsibility as a condition for a new order of regenerative societies. It is not only a new consciousness, it calls for a new social order.

It is worth pausing for a moment to recall a conversation with an indigenous elder who has a role as kaitiaki, a specific custodial or guardian role. The conversation reveals intra-activity in nature, in this case in the phenomena of water. We took a group on an observational walk along a river in his tribal area. As we walked we observed the impacts of bulldozers that had been used to remove the willow trees from the adjacent land, leaving the ground barren and exposed and denuding the river of its protective 'skin' and shade. Willow trees are deemed as invasive and damaging to the river ecosystem.

This intervention transgressed the ecological integrity of the river. The cooling effects of trees on the dynamics of water and sedimentation had not been accounted for. The erosion along the river banks was evident, as was the destruction of native trees, and the signs of algal blooms from water exposed to the sun. Our guide proclaimed 'water has consciousness.' I inquired further. 'Water has intelligence. The behavior of the river will change to respond to the light and heat and loss of root systems' (Te Rangiita, R. 2013).

Understanding the river in this way illustrates Barad's notion of intra-active phenomena—of the river with its surrounding ecology and with human relationship with the river's life. Barad notes

> Nature is not mute, and culture the articulate one. Nature writes, scribbles, experiments, calculates, thinks, breathes and laughs. (Barad, 2010, p. 268)

This understanding of intra-activity as constitutive of all matter with the interplay of physical and symbolic realms poses questions about knowledge that have particular cogency in the field of education for sustainability.

Education, Learning, Responsibility for Sustainable Sociality

A Levinasian approach to knowledge is enriched by Barad's view of the material and the discursive as intra-active: 'the material and the discursive are mutually implicated in the dynamics of intra—activity' (Barad, 2003, p. 822). An intra-active approach and a recognition of transcendence can be seen in the indigenous concept of a woven universe and in indigenous rituals of welcome where the world of light and understanding *and* the worlds beyond knowing, beyond time and comprehension, are acknowledged and addressed.

Levinas' account of knowledge is a critique of the mastery of knowing, whereas in Barad's and indigenous thought, knowledge is not an external entity, discrete from the knower or from the dynamic process of its production. The knower is not external to the world, nor exactly located in the world. Knowing comes from a process of participation in the co-evolution of the world 'we are part of the world in its ongoing intra-activity.' (ibid., p. 828) There is an affinity in all these approaches to knowledge as an infinite process.

The best theory and practice of education for sustainability carries some of the impetus and approach to knowledge outlined here. The aspiration of complex systems thinking and transformative learning keep open the dimension of transcendence, and refuse the impetus to systematic unity of thought and theory which signals totality. 'Responseability' in the performative reality of education means to keep alive the dimension of questioning, the 'prophetic,' to refuse the appropriation of knowledge to 'enhance the freedom of the satisfied man' (Levinas, 1996e, p. 153). To reduce the Other to 'presence' means in temporal terms, to lose the infinite quality of alterity, whether of the other person or the other as any form of matter, or knowledge. Strangely, the infinite is also proximate, inviting responsibility and relationality in all matters.

To approach knowledge of the biosphere responsibly is not to curtail the quest to understand the climate and human impacts on the planetary order as we know it, but to approach the quest for knowledge in respect for an ethical dimension, without anticipation of mastery, and with a willingness to be taught.

Levinas speaks to the imperative of going beyond systems of knowledge which underlie the exploitative character of the technology era:

> Even before the technology ascendency over things which knowledge of the industrial era has made possible and even before the technological development of modernity, knowledge by itself is the incarnate practice of seizure .... (Levinas, 1996e, p. 152)

When Levinas proposes a sociality that 'is no longer a simple aim but responsibility for the neighbor' (ibid., p. 158), he evokes the impetus of new principles and references as exemplified in education for sustainability. Education for sustainability has something of these attributes in its knowledge systems, in institutional initiatives, and policy. It is a notion with which mainstream systems are institutionally and conceptually out of synch (Royal, 2003, pp. 24–53). It is more in tune with the indigenous obligations to coming generations. Sustainability is a form of justice intended to support a sociality which recognizes that all forms of life are interconnected and intra-active across time spans.

Institutional initiatives for sustainability occupy an 'agonistic' position in education: one example of the tension between conventional systems of education, which emphasise competitive principles and holistic, collaborative, interdisciplinary can be seen in the global network of Regional Centers of Expertise (RCE's), implemented for the decade of Education for Sustainable Development. These sit uneasily with conventional structures of education. The orientation of RCE's is to form a learning community, a willingness to be taught generated through collaboration. Universities, schools, local government, business, and civil society organizations join in practices of responsibility through which knowledge is generated, yet they sit outside conventional systems and categories of knowledge (Martin, Shand, Hoskins, & Humphries, 2013).

At Oberlin College, Ohio, the curriculum is embedded in the buildings constructed with student and community involvement in the design, with non-toxic materials and renewable energy systems. The impetus of transformative education is that healthy sustainable systems are self-organizing, self-healing, and self-renewing—autonomy is sustained in relation to integrative parts of larger systems (Sterling, 2001, p. 54).

An environmental organization in New Zealand is considering adopting a constitutional proposal to keep a voice for the environment in decision-making. Attention to this voice will deepen the capacity of the organization to receive guidance for decision-making from the natural world itself. It signals a shift from the authority of human knowledge for environmental decision-making.

One of the hallmarks of transformative education for sustainability is experiential learning along the lines of the walk along the river. At a more systematic level, learning experiences designed to involve students in business, farming, and local government gives opportunities for practice and reflection that questions the systems of production and consumption to discern human and ecological impacts (Humphries

& Dey, 2014). Innovations in earth and eco-pedagogies and Earth Charter education take education outside the classroom to schools and neighborhoods and homes (Clugston, 2010) to learn to 'care for the fabric of life' (Capra, 1996 cited in Gadotti, 2010).

In Rhode Street School in New Zealand, children cook the food they grow for school lunches and take produce to sell at the market, so that economics become integrated with land and stream management. Moacir Gadotti refers to the garden as the curriculum:

> [S]eeing the seed assume the form of a plant and the plant assume the form of food, food that gives us life. In gardening we learn that things are not ready made, it is being made; it is making us; (Gadotti, 2010, p. 208)

The industrial project has been developed through a collective estrangement from the 'world' of nature, and education for sustainability is one of the healing threads.

Conclusion

Levinasian performative ethics of responsibility is taken to a different register by Barad's exposition of the intra-activity of all forms of life, which in turn deepens the impetus to a worldview of a woven universe. Education for sustainability is one area that activates a move toward this worldview with ecological and whole systems approaches and the aspiration for transformative learning.

With the locus of ethics in the *Same face-to face with an Other*, we do not need to labor over whether nature has a face; there are no parallel attempts to argue whether knowledge has a face! For Levinas, knowledge is transcendent in the same way as the face of the Other is transcendent. While the ambiguity of the face has been tantalizing to some, Levinas' persistence with the enigmatic quality of the Other is precisely because the Other cannot be defined. In the twenty-first century, we are faced with a new order of disturbance, and being brought into question by events of climate and the impacts on rivers and oceans and atmosphere and on humans, we are struggling to respond.

Acts of hospitality show something of interdependence; a gesture of kindness such as in the offering of water entangles us in the world that sustains life. Earth, water, and air, animals and plants are all matters for ethical encounter. It is a pivotal ontological move to place humans within the larger dynamics of the planet, of which humans are only one life form. If the social contract of freedom (from constraint), autonomy, and private property ownership is to shift to a sociality arising from being-for-the-other, then le *tiers* the arena of sociality will provide for the full dimensions of existence.

Climate change is calling us into question. It exposes the impoverishment of social industrial systems premised on the grasp of knowledge; it puts in question freedom that escapes accountability for destroying the balance of climate system—this is an instance of injustice harbored by freedom. To restore the interwoven fabric of life and matter, we will need to be taught by the world of nature and discover transcendence in new dimensions of responsibility.

At its best, education for sustainability could shape things to come: we are inescapably intra-acting and response-able, weaving the world together and apart regardless of which

LEVINAS AND THE PHILOSOPHY OF EDUCATION

trajectory this takes. Response-ability contributes to the shaping of things in favor of regenerating the planet in its interwoven complexity.

A final abrupt word from Levinas speaks wonderfully of responsibility as more than conscience: 'the truth of transcendence consists in the concordance of speech with acts' (Levinas, 1996d, p. 76).

Disclosure statement

No potential conflict of interest was reported by the author.

References

Barad, K. (2003). Posthumanist performativity: Toward an understanding of how matter comes to matter. *Signs: Journal of Women in Culture and Society, 28,* 801–831. Gender and Science: New Issues.

Barad, K. (2007). *Meeting the universe halfway.* Durham: Duke University Press.

Barad, K. (2010). Quantum entanglements and hauntological relations of inheritance: Dis/continuities, spacetime enfoldings and justice-to-come. In *Derrida Today* (pp. 240–268). Edinburgh University Press. Retrieved from www.eupjournals.com/drt

Berkes, F., Colding, J., & Folke, C. (Eds.). (2003). *Navigating social – ecological systems.* Cambridge: Cambridge University Press.

Calame, P. (2009). *Essay on oeconomy.* The original title 'Essai sur l'oeconomie'. Paris: Editions Charles-Léopold Mayer.

Calame, P. with Sizoo, E. (2012). AFTER RIO + 20. *Making responsibility the ethical core of the twenty-first century.* Retrieved from http://www.response.org.nz/resources-2/

Clugston, R. (2010, September). Introduction: Earth charter education for sustainable ways of living. *Journal of Education for Sustainable Development, 4.*

Critchley, S. (1992). *The ethics of deconstruction: Derrida and Levinas.* Oxford: Blackwell.

De Boer, T. (1986). An ethical transcendental philosophy. In R. Cohen (Ed.), *Face to face with Levinas* (pp. 83–116). Albany: State University of New York Press.

Gadotti, M. (2010). Reorienting education practices towards sustainability. In R. Clugston & M. Vilela (Eds.), Special issue to mark ten years of the earth charter (pp. 203–418). *Journal of Education for Sustainable Development, 4.* Los Angeles: Sage.

Grinlinton, D., & Taylor, P. (Eds.). (2011). *Property rights and sustainability.* Leiden: Koninklijke Brill NV.

Hall, S. (1986). Variants of liberalism. In L. Donald & S. Hall (Eds.), *Politics and idealogy* (pp. 34–115). Milton Keynes: Open University Press.

Hoskins, T. K. (2010). *Māori and Levinas. Kanohi ki te Kanohi for an Ethical Politics* (PhD Thesis). University of Auckland, New Zealand.

Hoskins, T. K., Martin, B., & Humphries, M. (2011). The power of relational responsibility. *EJBO, 16,* 22–27. *EJBO Electronic Journal of Business Ethics and Organization Studies.* Retrieved from https://jyx.jyu.fi/dspace/handle/123456789/37277

Humphries, M., & Dey, K. (2014). *'Elephant in the paddock.'* Paper for CR3+ Conference, Melbourne, Australia.

LEVINAS AND THE PHILOSOPHY OF EDUCATION

Levinas, E. (1969). *Totality and infinity*. (A. Lingis, Trans.) (pp. 13–34). Pittsburgh, PA: Duquesne University Press.

Levinas, E. (1986). Dialogue with Emmanuel Levinas and Richard Kearney. In R. A. Cohen (Ed.), *Face to face with Levinas*. Albany: State University of New York Press.

Levinas, E. (1987). *Collected philosophical papers*. (A. Lingis, Trans.). Pittsburgh, PA: Duquesne University Press.

Levinas, E. (1996a). 'Transcendence and height'. In A. T. Peperzak, S. Critchey, & R. Bernasconi (Eds.), *Emanuel Levinas. Basic philosophical writings* (pp. 11–32). Bloomington and Indianapolis, IA: Indiana University Press.

Levinas, E. (1996b). 'Peace and proximity'. In A. T. Peperzak, S. Critchey, & R. Bernasconi (Eds.), *Emanuel Levinas. Basic philosophical writings* (pp. 161–170). Bloomington and Indianapolis, IA: Indiana University Press.

Levinas, E. (1996c). 'Is ontology fundamental?' In A. T. Peperzak, S. Critchey, & R. Bernasconi (Eds.), *Emanuel Levinas. Basic philosophical writings* (pp. 1–10). Bloomington and Indianapolis, IA: Indiana University Press.

Levinas, E. (1996d). 'Enigma and phenomenon'. In A. T. Peperzak, S. Critchey, & R. Bernasconi (Eds.), *Emanuel Levinas. Basic philosophical writings* (pp. 65–77). Bloomington and Indianapolis, IA: Indiana University Press.

Levinas, E. (1996e). 'Transcendence and intelligibility'. In A. T. Peperzak, S. Critchey, & R. Bernasconi (Eds.), *Emanuel Levinas. Basic philosophical writings* (pp. 149–159). Bloomington and Indianapolis, IA: Indiana University Press.

Levinas, E. (2009). *Otherwise than being or beyond essence*. (A. Lingis, Trans.). Pittsburgh, PA: Dusquesne University Press.

Llewelyn, J. (1991). Am I obsessed by Bobby (Humanism of the other Animal). In R. Bernasconi & S. Critchley (Eds.), *Re-reading Levinas* (pp. 11–49). Bloomington: Indiana University Press.

Martin, B. (2014, February). *An ethics of responsibility in law: Considerations from Emmanuel Levinas*. Paper presented to New Thinking for Sustainability, Earth Law Conference, Wellington, New Zealand. Submitted to Special Issue of the New Zealand Journal of Public and International Law.

Martin, B., Shand, D., Hoskins, Te. K., & Humphries, M. (2013). *Sustaining people and planet*. Retrieved from http://www.response.org.nz/resources-2/

Perpich, D. (2008). *The Ethics of Emmanuel Levinas*. Stanford, CA: Stanford University Press.

Royal, T. A. C. (Ed.). (2003). *The woven universe*. Edited Writings of Revd. Māori Marsden. Wellington: Marsden Estate.

Royal, C. T. A., & Martin, B. (2010). Indigenous ethics of responsibility in Aotearoa New Zealand. Harmony with the earth and relational ethics. In E. Sizoo (Ed.), *Responsibility and cultures of the world* (pp. 47–64). Berlin: P.I.E. Peter Lang.

Salmond, A. (2012). Ontological quarrels: Indigeneity, exclusion and citizenship in a relational world. *Anthropological Theory, 12*, 115–141. Sage.

Sizoo, E. (2010). *Responsibility and cultures of the world*. Berlin: P.I.E. Peter Lang.

Sterling, S. (2001). *Sustainable education* (Schumacher Briefing No. 6). Totnes, Devon: Green Books for the Schumacher Society.

Te Rangiita, R. (2013) *Personal communication*. Turangi.

Tunks, A. (2013). 'One indigenous vision for sustainable law? Tensions and prospects. In K. Bosslemann & D. Grinlinton (Eds.), *Environmental law for a sustainable society* (pp. 97–121). Champaign, IL: Wiley-Blackwell.

Zhao, G. (2012). Levinas and the mission of education. In *Educational Theory* (pp. 659–674, Vol. 62, No. 6). Board of Trustees, University of Illinois.

Index

Note: Page numbers followed by 'n' refer to notes

absolute difference, language 38
abstraction, concrete 44
adaptation, learning 56–7
Ahmed, S. 89
alimentation 91
alter ego 43
alterity, infinite 109
anthropology, hermeneutical 57
anti-Platoism 58
anti-totalitarianism 1, 25
authoritarian, teaching 54, 66
autonomy 15

Barad, K. 98, 106, 107, 109, 111
Bauman, Z. 55
Beatty, J. 33
Being 41
Being and Time (Heidegger) 48
Bergo, B. 88, 91
Bergson, H., duration 75
Bhambra, G. K. 9, 10
Biesta, G. 3, 5–6, 26, 31, 52–70
biosphere 110
Blanchot, M. 27–8
bodies, as modes 86
bodily sensations, cultural practices 89
British history 9–10
Buber, M. 33

Cavell, S. 16
Caygill, H. 11, 14–15, 17–18
challenge, consciousness 62
Charlie Hebdo (magazine), attack (Jan 2015)
   20
Chinnery, A. 26, 35
citizenship education 13
Clarke, K. 10
climate change 111
colonialism 15
colonization 98

commonplaces 16
communication 62
communicative theory (Habermas) 26,
   30, 34
community 15, 20; democracy and education
   34–6; ethical multiplicity 28; ethical nature
   26; human 26, 34; inoperative 25; language
   building 30; language-bond 29; Levinas 34;
   notions of 25; rational 26; responsibility 34;
   singularities 24–37; without community 25
community and education, philosophical
   developments 25–7
concrete abstraction 44
consciousness 72, 73, 87, 93n5; challenge 62
constructivism 71–4; reconstructing
   temporally 75–7
consumption 42
control, teaching 65
cosmopolitanism 10
Critchley, S. 100, 102, 103
critical thinking 49
cultural practices, bodily sensations 89
cultural significations, multiplicity 59

De Boer, T. 102
deformalization 61
Deleuze, G. 85, 86, 88
democracy 4, 34–6; ethical community 34–5;
   Habermas 30; singularity and community
   24–37
Democracy and Education (Dewey) 35
Derrida, J. 25, 38, 47, 48, 50n3, 50n6, 59;
   criticism of Levinas 73–4
Descartes, R., *Meditations* 40
desire 60–2
Dewey, J. 53, 57; *Democracy and Education* 35
diachronic time 81
diachrony 79
dialog, listening 32–3
difference 1, 30; absolute 38; schools 25

INDEX

Difficult Freedom (Levinas) 2, 13
discourse, language 29–30
Dreyfus Affair 11–12, 22n3
duration (Bergson) 75
Durkheim, E. 4; *Individualism and the Intellectuals* 12; influence of 9–23; moral education lectures (1902) 13; organic solidarity 11, 17; patriotism 20

Eaglestone, R. 15
Earth Charter education 111
eco-pedagogy 7
École Normale Israélite Orientale, Levinas as Director 19
economic signification 59
economic time 77, 80
economics, environment 97
education: citizenship 13; and community 25–7; community and democracy 34–6; ethics 9–23; incarnate 83–95; learning-centered 56, 71–82; sustainability 111
Education for Sustainable Development 110
ego 62, 77; freedom 76; knowing 72–3; Other 60
ego-object 67
egoism 28, 97
egological world view, overcoming 55–6
embodiment: materiality and transcendence 87–92; pedagogical question 85–7
empathy 101
engagement, responsibility 101
Enlightenment 40
environment, economics 97
equality 14, 15
ethical command 44
ethical community, democracy 34–5
ethical multiplicity, community 28
ethical nature, community 26
ethics 62–65; education 9–23; everyday life 11; philosophy 13; postmodernism 2; of worlding 107
ethics and knowledge, quantum dynamics 106–7
ethology 86
everyday ethics, education 19–21
everyday life 11
exclusionary politics, history 10
Existence and Existents (Levinas) 42, 45
experience, sensory 47–8

face 43, 47, 62, 84; beyond human 99; epiphany 61; language 38–39, 45; sound of 44–9
false identity thinking, totalitarianism 1
fascism 25
form of life 16

fraternity 12, 15, 17, 22n4; prophetic politics 18
free speech 20
freedom 63–4; ego 76; hostage 102–3; other 28; responsibility 14, 96
future 78

Gadotti, M. 111
Gallop, J. 86
gift: of teaching 4; of time 78
given 41, 50n1
goose bump effect (Probyn) 86, 89
Gove, M. 9
Grayling, T. 10
Grossman, V., *Life and Fate* 43–4

Habermas, J.: communicative theory 26, 30, 34; democracy 30
Haroutunian-Gordon, S. 33; and Laverty, M. J. 32
hau 105, 108
Havel, V. 20–1
Hegel, H., *The Science of Logic* 30–1
Heidegger, M. 14, 41, 43, 68n8, 68n9; *Being and Time* 48
hermeneutical anthropology 57
hermeneutical world view 56–8
heteronomy 83
history: exclusionary politics 10; immigration 9–10; politics of present 9
Hitlerism 14, 19
horizontal form of life 16
Hoskins, K. 105
hostage, freedom 102–3
human community 26, 34
Human Rights 10
human-centered responsibility 97–8
humanism 67–8n3
humans, quantum dynamics 106
Husserl, E. 14, 40–3, 61, 76

I, Māori 105
idealism, transcendental 14, 20
identity 107; phenomena 107
illeity 17
immanence 58; subjectivity 64
immigration, history 9–10
inclusion, radical 20
indigenous societal systems 105–6
indigenous thought 98
individualism, moral 12
Individualism and the Intellectuals (Durkheim) 12
infinite alterity 109
infinite unknowing, teaching relation 102–3
influence 2
instant, redemption of 78

INDEX

interdependence 111
interlocutor, Other 60
International Alliance for Responsible and Sustainable Societies 7
intra-activity, nature 109
invisibility 88–9
Irigaray, L. 87
Is it Righteous to Be? (Levinas) 19
Is Ontology Fundamental? (Levinas) 107

Joldersma, C. 6, 71–82
Judaism 19
justice 103–4; society 13–19

knowing ego 72–3
knowledge 40, 103; and ethics 106–7

language: absolute difference 38; building community 30; discourse 29–30; face 38–9, 45; as speech 46
Laverty, M. J., and Haroutunian-Gordon, S. 32
learning: adaptation 56–7; environments 56–8; meaning-making 65
learning-centered education 56, 71–82
Levinas, E.: École Normale Israélite Orientale Director 19; influence 2; three waves of scholarship 84
Levinas and Education: At the Intersection of Faith and Reason (Ed. Égea-Kuehene) 2
liberalism 15, 97
Life and Fate (Grossman) 43–4
Lighart, J. 53
light: rays of 39–42; sound 38–51
Lingis, A. 16, 26, 31
listener, good 33
listening 32–4
liturgy 60–2
Llewelyn, J. 99
logos 46
Luhmann, N. 57

Māori society, obligation 98, 105
Martin, B. 6–7, 96–113
materialism 59
materiality 85; transcendence and embodiment 87–92
matter 106
Maturana, H., and Varela, F. 57
May, T. 2, 10; and difference 25, 28, 30
Meaning and Sense 58–60
meaning-making, learning 65
Meditations (Descartes) 40
Meirieu, P. 52, 54, 67
Merleau-Ponty, M. 48
metaphors: spatial 72–4; visual 32
minorities 20

modernity, Republican 11–13
modernization 13
moral, and the social 13
moral education lectures (Durkheim, 1902) 13
moral individualism 12
moral nature, social life 11
moral obligation 16, 32
morality 61
multiplicity: maintaining genuine 27; singularity 24, 27–9

Nancy, J.-L. 25
National Socialism 13–14
nature: intra-activity 109; is the Other 108
Nazism 25
need 60–2
Nemo, P. 11
neoliberalism 11
nihilism 2
Nordtug, B. 2

obedience 64
objectivity 16
obligation 16; Māori society 98; moral 16, 32
ontology 100–1, 107
organic solidarity (Durkheim) 12, 17
Other 84; ego 60; ethics 100; freedom 28; interlocutor 60, 61; Nature is the 108; phenomenon 61; refusal of engagement with 59; relation 43–4; responsibility for 97; and the Same 101; and self 15; teacher as 71–82; unknowability 90
Otherness 15; responsibility 26
Otherwise than Being (Levinas) 14, 17–18, 46, 87–8, 91, 98

page 5, 39
patriotism 20
Peace and Proximity (Levinas) 100
Perpich, D. 90, 99–100, 101
phenomena: identities 107; interactive 109; Other 61
philosophy, ethics 13
plasticity 92
Plato 40, 58; *Symposium* 33
pluralism 27
political violence 14
politics: exclusionary 10; prophetic 13–19
postmodernism 2
pragmatism 68n4
precariousness 100
principles of '89 (radical republicanism) 11
private choice, public good 20
privileged culture, of Plato 58
Probyn, E. 86–7, 89
prophetic politics 13–19; fraternity 18
proximity 100

INDEX

public good, private choice 20

quantum dynamics: ethics and knowledge
106–7; humans 106; link to Levinas and
ethics 107–9

racism 91
radical republicanism 11
Radicalizing Levinas (Eds. Atterton and
Calarco) 94
rational agents 26
rational community 26
Reflections on the Philosophy of Hitlerism
(Levinas) 14, 15
relating singularities 29–30
relation, without relation 27–8
relativism 2
Republican modernity 11–13
response-ability 106, 112
responsibility 55; community 34; engagement
101; face and scope 99–100; freedom 14,
96; human-centered 97–8; Levinas for
21st Century 96–113; mundane 19; for
Other 97; otherness 26; radical 100–2;
subjectivity 17; sustainable sociality
109–11
responsivity 15
Revelation, Jewish tradition 62–5
Richardson, V. 53
Rikowski, G. 2
ritualization, sacred 18
robot vacuum cleaners 56–8

sacred, ritualization 18
Salmond, A. 105
Same, and the Other 101
sameness 15
Sartre, J. -P. 41
saying 46
scholarship, three ways of (Levinas) 84
schools, differences 25
Science of Logic, The (Hegel) 30–1
self, and other 15
self-interest 97
self-subject 67
self–Other relation 88
Sellars, W. 50n1
sensation 83, 88, 89, 90
sense-making 59, 64
sensibility 87, 88
sensible, immediacy of 91
sensible transcendence 92
sensory experience 47–8
Severson, E., on *Totality and Infinity*
73–6
signification, economic 59
Signification and Sense (Levinas) 58–60

signs 47
singularities: community 24–37, 30–4;
multiplicity 24, 27–9; relating 29–30;
subjectivity 28
the social 12
social: and the moral 13; obligation to others
17; transcendent 20; understanding 12
social life, moral nature 11
sociality, sustainable 109–11
societal systems, indigenous 105–6
society 13; justice 13–19
solidarity 101; organic 12, 17
sound: face of 44–9; light 38–51
Sparrow, T. 85, 88, 89, 91–2, 93n4
speaking 30–1
speech: language as 46; thought is 38, 48
Standish, P. 18; and Williams, E. 5, 38–51
Strhan, A. 4, 9–23, 29
student-subject 67
subjectivity 3, 88; alchemy of 87; ethics 55;
immanence 64; irreducible 27; responsibility
17; singularity 28
subjectness 54–5, 67n2, 67n3
subordination, intellect 58
sustainability 98; education 110, 111
sustainable sociality, responsibility 109–11
Symposium (Plato) 33

teacher: Other 71–82; transcendence 71–82; as
transcendent (spatial metaphors) 72–4
teaching 68n12; authoritarian 54, 66; control
65; gift of 4; rediscovery 52–70; systemizing
teaching and learning 87; transmission
model 53; what is actually wrong with
traditional 53–5
teaching relation, infinite unknowing 102–3
things 42, 50n3
thinking: critical 49; false identity 1; skills
49–50
thought: elements of 38–51; indigenous 98; is
speech 38, 48
thought process, traditional 40
thought-qua-light 42–3
thought-qua-sound 48
time 77, 79; diachronic 81; economic 77, 80;
gift 78
Todd, S. 3–4, 6, 26, 34, 83–95
totalitarianism 25; false identity thinking 1
totality 28; language 29; listening 34
Totality and Infinity (Levinas) 2, 14, 15, 26, 27,
83; Severson on 73–6
totalization 15–16, 16, 20
transcendence 55, 62–5, 112; embodiment
and materiality 87–92; problem with 90;
sensible 92; teacher 71–82
transcendent: temporalizing 77–9;
temporalizing teacher as 79–81

INDEX

transcendental idealism 14; social 20
transmission model, teaching 53
truth 19

unknowing 102–3

Varela, F., and Maturana, H. 57
vertical form of life 16
visual metaphors 32
von Glasersfeld, E. 72

vulnerability 91

Waks, L. J. 32
Williams, E., and Standish, P. 5, 38–51
Wittgenstein, L. 16
Work 61; Other-centered 59
world view, hermeneutical 56–8
worlding, ethics 107

Zhao, G. 1–8, 24–37, 104